Monitoring Hadoop

Get to grips with the intricacies of Hadoop monitoring using the power of Ganglia and Nagios

Gurmukh Singh

BIRMINGHAM - MUMBAI

Monitoring Hadoop

Copyright © 2015 Packt Publishing

All rights reserved. No part of this book may be reproduced, stored in a retrieval system, or transmitted in any form or by any means, without the prior written permission of the publisher, except in the case of brief quotations embedded in critical articles or reviews.

Every effort has been made in the preparation of this book to ensure the accuracy of the information presented. However, the information contained in this book is sold without warranty, either express or implied. Neither the author, nor Packt Publishing, and its dealers and distributors will be held liable for any damages caused or alleged to be caused directly or indirectly by this book.

Packt Publishing has endeavored to provide trademark information about all of the companies and products mentioned in this book by the appropriate use of capitals. However, Packt Publishing cannot guarantee the accuracy of this information.

First published: April 2015

Production reference: 1240415

Published by Packt Publishing Ltd.
Livery Place
35 Livery Street
Birmingham B3 2PB, UK.

ISBN 978-1-78328-155-8

www.packtpub.com

Credits

Author
Gurmukh Singh

Reviewers
David Greco
Randal Scott King
Yousuf Qureshi

Acquisition Editor
Meeta Rajani

Content Development Editor
Siddhesh Salvi

Technical Editor
Parag Topre

Copy Editors
Hiral Bhat
Sarang Chari
Tani Kothari
Trishla Singh

Project Coordinator
Nidhi Joshi

Proofreaders
Safis Editing
Paul Hindle

Indexer
Hemangini Bari

Graphics
Disha Haria

Production Coordinator
Melwyn D'sa

Cover Work
Melwyn D'sa

About the Author

Gurmukh Singh has been an infrastructure engineer for over 10 years and has worked on big data platforms in the past 5 years. He started his career as a field engineer, setting up lease lines and radio links. He has vast experience in enterprise servers and network design and in scaling infrastructures and tuning them for performance. He is the founder of a small start-up called Netxillon Technologies, which is into big data training and consultancy. He talks at various technical meetings and is an active participant in the open source community's activities. He writes at `http://linuxaddict.org` and maintains his Github account at `https://github.com/gdhillon`.

About the Reviewers

David Greco is a software architect with more than 27 years of experience. He started his career as a researcher in the field of high-performance computing; thereafter, he moved to the business world, where he worked for different enterprise software vendors and two start-ups he helped create. He played different roles, those of a consultant and software architect and even a CTO. He's an enthusiastic explorer of new technologies, and he likes to introduce new technologies into enterprises to improve their businesses. In the past 5 years, he has fallen in love with big data technologies and typed functional programming—Scala and Haskell. When not working or hacking, he likes to practice karate and listen to jazz and classical music.

Randal Scott King is the managing partner of Brilliant Data, a global consultancy specializing in big data, analytics, and network architecture. He has done work for industry-leading clients, such as Sprint, Lowe's Home Improvement, Gulfstream Aerospace, and AT&T. In addition to the current book, he was previously a reviewer for *Hadoop MapReduce v2 Cookbook*, *Second Edition*, *Packt Publishing*.

Scott lives with his children on the outskirts of Atlanta, GA. You can visit his blog at www.randalscottking.com.

Yousuf Qureshi is an early adopter of technology and gadgets, has a lot of experience in the e-commerce, social media, analytics, and mobile apps sectors, and is a Cloudera Certified Developer for Apache Hadoop (CCDH).

His expertise includes development, technology turnaround, consultancy, and architecture. He is an experienced developer of Android, iOS, Blackberry, ASP.NET MVC, Java, MapReduce, Distributed Search and Inverted Index algorithms, Hadoop, Hive, Apache Pig, Media API integration, and multiplatform applications. He has also reviewed *Instant jQuery Drag-and-Drop Grids How-to*, *Packt Publishing*, earlier.

> Special thanks go to my, wife Shakira Yousuf, and daughter, Inaaya Yousuf.

www.PacktPub.com

Support files, eBooks, discount offers, and more

For support files and downloads related to your book, please visit www.PacktPub.com.

Did you know that Packt offers eBook versions of every book published, with PDF and ePub files available? You can upgrade to the eBook version at www.PacktPub.com and as a print book customer, you are entitled to a discount on the eBook copy. Get in touch with us at service@packtpub.com for more details.

At www.PacktPub.com, you can also read a collection of free technical articles, sign up for a range of free newsletters and receive exclusive discounts and offers on Packt books and eBooks.

https://www2.packtpub.com/books/subscription/packtlib

Do you need instant solutions to your IT questions? PacktLib is Packt's online digital book library. Here, you can search, access, and read Packt's entire library of books.

Why subscribe?

- Fully searchable across every book published by Packt
- Copy and paste, print, and bookmark content
- On demand and accessible via a web browser

Free access for Packt account holders

If you have an account with Packt at www.PacktPub.com, you can use this to access PacktLib today and view 9 entirely free books. Simply use your login credentials for immediate access.

Table of Contents

Preface	**v**
Chapter 1: Introduction to Monitoring	**1**
The need for monitoring	**2**
The monitoring tools available in the market	**2**
Nagios	3
Nagios architecture	3
Prerequisites for installing and configuring Nagios	3
Installing Nagios	4
Web interface configuration	5
Nagios plugins	7
Verification	7
Configuration files	7
Setting up monitoring for clients	8
Ganglia	11
Ganglia components	11
Ganglia installation	12
System logging	**14**
Collection	14
Transportation	14
Storage	14
Alerting and analysis	14
The syslogd and rsyslogd daemons	15
Summary	**16**
Chapter 2: Hadoop Daemons and Services	**17**
Hadoop daemons	**18**
NameNode	18
DataNode and TaskTracker	19
Secondary NameNode	20
JobTracker and YARN daemons	20
The communication between daemons	21

Table of Contents

YARN framework	**23**
Common issues faced on Hadoop cluster	24
Host-level checks	25
Nagios server	26
Configuring Hadoop nodes for monitoring	27
Summary	**28**
Chapter 3: Hadoop Logging	**29**
The need for logging events	**30**
System logging	**30**
Logging levels	**31**
Logging in Hadoop	**32**
Hadoop logs	33
Hadoop log level	34
Hadoop audit	35
Summary	**36**
Chapter 4: HDFS Checks	**37**
HDFS overview	**38**
Nagios master configuration	**39**
The Nagios client configuration	**43**
Summary	**44**
Chapter 5: MapReduce Checks	**45**
MapReduce overview	**46**
MapReduce control commands	**46**
MapReduce health checks	**48**
Nagios master configuration	**48**
Nagios client configuration	**52**
Summary	**52**
Chapter 6: Hadoop Metrics and Visualization Using Ganglia	**53**
Hadoop metrics	**54**
Metrics contexts	**54**
Named contexts	54
Metrics system design	**55**
Metrics configuration	**56**
Configuring Metrics2	**57**
Exploring the metrics contexts	**59**
Hadoop Ganglia integration	**59**
Hadoop metrics configuration for Ganglia	60
Setting up Ganglia nodes	61

Hadoop configuration	**62**
Metrics1	62
Metrics2	63
Ganglia graphs	**64**
Metrics APIs	**64**
The org.apache.hadoop.metrics package	64
The org.apache.hadoop.metrics2 package	65
Summary	**65**
Chapter 7: Hive, HBase, and Monitoring Best Practices	**67**
Hive monitoring	**67**
Hive metrics	**68**
HBase monitoring	69
HBase Nagios monitoring	**69**
HBase metrics	**71**
Monitoring best practices	**73**
The Filter class	**74**
Nagios and Ganglia best practices	**74**
Summary	**75**
Index	**77**

Preface

Many organizations are implementing Hadoop in production environments, storing critical data on it, and making sure everything is in place and running as desired as it is crucial for the business. If something breaks down, how quickly you can detect it and remediate it is very important. In order to have early detection of any failures, there is a need to have monitoring in place and capture events that let you peep into the internal workings of a Hadoop cluster. The goal of this book is to enable monitoring and capture events to make sure that the Hadoop clusters are up and running to the optimal capacity.

What this book covers

Chapter 1, *Introduction to Monitoring*, discusses the need for monitoring and the tools available in the market for that. This chapter also provides details about installing Nagios and Ganglia, which are the tools to monitor and capture metrics for a Hadoop cluster.

Chapter 2, *Hadoop Daemons and Services*, discusses the Hadoop services and daemons and how they communicate. Before implementing monitoring, one must understand how Hadoop components talk to each other and what ports the services run on.

Chapter 3, *Hadoop Logging*, discusses how system logging works and how that extends to logging in Hadoop clusters. This chapter also covers the logging details for various Hadoop daemons.

Chapter 4, *HDFS Checks*, explores the HDFS checks, which can be implemented for Hadoop File System and its components, such as NameNode, DataNode, and so on.

Chapter 5, *MapReduce Checks*, discusses configuring checks for MapReduce components, such as JobTracker, TaskTracker, ResourceManager, and other YARN components.

Preface

Chapter 6, *Hadoop Metrics and Visualization Using Ganglia*, provides a step-by-step guide to configuring a Hadoop metrics collection and its visualization using Ganglia.

Chapter 7, *Hive, HBase, and Monitoring Best Practices*, provides an introduction to metrics collection and monitoring for the Hive and HBase components of the Hadoop framework. It also talks about the best practices for monitoring on a large scale and how to keep the utilization of the monitoring servers optimized.

What you need for this book

To practice the examples provided in this book, you will need a working Hadoop cluster. It is recommended that you use Cent OS 6.0 at the minimum and Apache Hadoop 1.2.1 and Hadoop 2.6.0 for the Hadoop version 1 and Hadoop version 2 examples, respectively.

Who this book is for

Monitoring Hadoop is ideal for Hadoop administrators who need to monitor their Hadoop clusters and make sure they are running optimally. This book acts as a reference to set up Hadoop monitoring and visualization using Ganglia.

Conventions

In this book, you will find a number of text styles that distinguish between different kinds of information. Here are some examples of these styles and an explanation of their meaning.

Code words in text, database table names, folder names, filenames, file extensions, pathnames, dummy URLs, user input, and Twitter handles are shown as follows: "This is the port for ResourceManager scheduler; the default is `8030`."

A block of code is set as follows:

```
log4j.appender.DRFAAUDIT=org.apache.log4j.DailyRollingFileAppender
log4j.appender.DRFAAUDIT.File=/var/log/audit.log
log4j.appender.DRFAAUDIT.DatePattern=.yyyy-MM-dd
log4j.appender.DRFAAUDIT.layout=org.apache.log4j.PatternLayout
```

When we wish to draw your attention to a particular part of a code block, the relevant lines or items are set in bold:

```
log4j.appender.DRFAAUDIT=org.apache.log4j.DailyRollingFileAppender
log4j.appender.DRFAAUDIT.File=/var/log/audit.log
log4j.appender.DRFAAUDIT.DatePattern=.yyyy-MM-dd
log4j.appender.DRFAAUDIT.layout=org.apache.log4j.PatternLayout
```

Any command-line input or output is written as follows:

```
$ sudo /usr/local/nagios/bin/nagios -v /usr/local/nagios/etc/nagios.cfg
```

New terms and **important words** are shown in bold. Words that you see on the screen, for example, in menus or dialog boxes, appear in the text like this: "If you see a message, such as **Return code of 127 is out of bounds - plugin may be missing** on the right panel, then this means that your configuration is correct as of now."

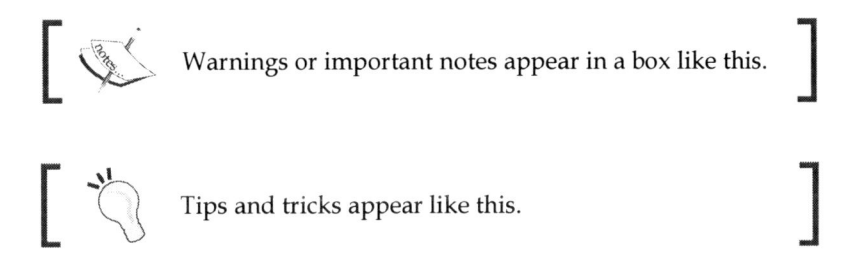

> Warnings or important notes appear in a box like this.

> Tips and tricks appear like this.

Reader feedback

Feedback from our readers is always welcome. Let us know what you think about this book—what you liked or disliked. Reader feedback is important for us as it helps us develop titles that you will really get the most out of.

To send us general feedback, simply e-mail feedback@packtpub.com, and mention the book's title in the subject of your message.

If there is a topic that you have expertise in and you are interested in either writing or contributing to a book, see our author guide at www.packtpub.com/authors.

Customer support

Now that you are the proud owner of a Packt book, we have a number of things to help you to get the most from your purchase.

Errata

Although we have taken every care to ensure the accuracy of our content, mistakes do happen. If you find a mistake in one of our books—maybe a mistake in the text or the code—we would be grateful if you could report this to us. By doing so, you can save other readers from frustration and help us improve subsequent versions of this book. If you find any errata, please report them by visiting http://www.packtpub.com/submit-errata, selecting your book, clicking on the **Errata Submission Form** link, and entering the details of your errata. Once your errata are verified, your submission will be accepted and the errata will be uploaded to our website or added to any list of existing errata under the Errata section of that title.

To view the previously submitted errata, go to https://www.packtpub.com/books/content/support and enter the name of the book in the search field. The required information will appear under the **Errata** section.

Piracy

Piracy of copyrighted material on the Internet is an ongoing problem across all media. At Packt, we take the protection of our copyright and licenses very seriously. If you come across any illegal copies of our works in any form on the Internet, please provide us with the location address or website name immediately so that we can pursue a remedy.

Please contact us at copyright@packtpub.com with a link to the suspected pirated material.

We appreciate your help in protecting our authors and our ability to bring you valuable content.

Questions

If you have a problem with any aspect of this book, you can contact us at questions@packtpub.com, and we will do our best to address the problem.

Introduction to Monitoring

In any enterprise, no matter how big or small, it is very important to monitor the health of all its components such as servers, network devices, databases, and so on, and make sure that things are working as intended. Monitoring is a critical part for any business that is dependent upon infrastructure. This can be done by giving signals to enable the necessary actions in case of any failures.

In a real production environment, monitoring can be very complex with many components and configurations. There might be different security zones, different ways in which servers are set up, or the same database might have been used in many different ways with servers listening to various service ports.

Before diving into setting up monitoring and logging for Hadoop, it is very important to understand the basics of monitoring, how it works, and some commonly used tools in the market. In Hadoop, we can monitor the resources, services, and also collect the metrics of various Hadoop counters. In this book, we will be looking at monitoring and metrics collection.

In this chapter, we will begin our journey by exploring the open source monitoring tools that we use in enterprises, and learn how to configure them.

The following topics will be covered in this chapter:

- Some of the widely used monitoring tools
- Installing and configuring Nagios
- Installing and configuring Ganglia
- Understanding how system logging works

The need for monitoring

If we have tested our code and found that the functionality and everything else is fine, then why do we need monitoring?

The production load might be different from what we tested and found, there could be human errors while conducting the day-to-days operations, someone could have executed a wrong command or added a wrong configuration. There could also be hardware/network failures that could make your application unavailable. How long can you afford to keep the application down? Maybe for a few minutes or for a few hours, but what about the revenue loss, or what if it is a critical application for carrying out financial transactions? We need to respond to the failures as soon as possible, and this can be done only if we perform early detections and send out notifications.

The monitoring tools available in the market

In the market, there are many tools are available for monitoring, but the important things to keep in mind are as follows:

- How easy it is to deploy and maintain the tool
- The license costs, but more importantly the **TCO (Total Cost of Ownership)**
- Can it perform standard checks, and how easy is to write custom plugins
- Overhead in terms of CPU and memory usage
- User interface

Some of the monitoring tools available in the market are BandwidthD, EasyNetMonitor, Zenoss, NetXMS, Splunk, and many more.

Of the many tools available, Nagios and Ganglia are most widely deployed for monitoring the Hadoop clusters. Many Hadoop vendors, such as Cloudera and Hortonworks use Nagios and Ganglia for monitoring their clusters.

Nagios

Nagios is a powerful monitoring system that provides you with instant awareness about your organization's mission-critical IT infrastructure.

By using Nagios, you can do the following:

- Plan the release cycle and the rollouts, before things are outdated
- Early detection, before it causes an outage
- Have automation and a better response across the organization
- Find hindrances in the infrastructure, which could impact the SLAs

Nagios architecture

The Nagios architecture was designed keeping in mind flexibility and scalability. It consists of a central server, which is referred to as the Monitoring Server and the clients are the Nagios agents, that run on each node that needs to be monitored.

The checks can be performed for service, port, memory, disk, and so on, by using either active checks or passive checks. The active checks are initiated by the Nagios server and the passive checks are initiated by the client. Its flexibility allows us to have programmable APIs and customizable plugins for monitoring.

Prerequisites for installing and configuring Nagios

Nagios is an enterprise class monitoring solution, which can manage a large number of nodes. It can be scaled easily, and it has the ability to write custom plugins for your applications. Nagios is quite flexible and powerful, and it supports many configurations and components.

 Nagios is such a vast and extensive product that this chapter is in no way a reference manual for it. This chapter is written with the primary aim of setting up monitoring, as quickly as possible, and familiarizing the readers with it.

Prerequisites

Always set up a separate host as the monitoring node/server and do not install other critical services on it. The number of hosts that are monitored can be a few thousand, with each host having from 15 to 20 checks that can be either active or passive.

Before starting with the installation of Nagios, make sure that **Apache HTTP Server version 2.0** is running and gcc and gd have been installed. Make sure that you are logged in as root or as with sudo privileges. Nagios runs on many platforms, such as RHEL, Fedora, Windows, CentOS; however, in this book we will use the CentOS 6.5 platform.

```
$ ps -ef | grep httpd
$ service httpd status
$ rpm -qa | grep gcc
$ rpm -qa | grep gd
```

Installing Nagios

Let's look at the installation of Nagios, and how we can set it up. The following steps are for Rhel, CentOS, Fedora, and Ubuntu:

- Download Nagios and the Nagios plugin from the Nagios repository, which can be found at http://www.nagios.org/download/.
- The latest stable version of Naigos at the time of writing this chapter was nagios-4.0.8.tar.gz.
- Create a Nagios user to manage the Nagios interface. You have to execute the commands as either root or with sudo privileges.
- You can download it either from http://sourceforge.net/ or from any other commercial site, but a few sites might ask for registration.

  ```
  $ sudo /usr/sbin/useradd -m nagios
  $ passwd nagios
  ```

- Create a new nagcmd group so that external commands can be submitted through the web interface.
- If you prefer, you can download the file directly into the user's home directory.

- Create a Nagios user and an Apache user, as a part of the group.

   ```
   $ sudo /usr/sbin/groupadd nagcmd
   $ sudo /usr/sbin/usermod -a -G nagcmd nagios
   $ sudo /usr/sbin/usermod -a -G nagcmd apache
   ```

Let's start with the configuration.

Navigate to the directory, where the package was downloaded. The downloaded package could be either in the Downloads folder or in the present working directory.

```
$ tar zxvf nagios-4.0.8.tar.gz
$ cd nagios-4.0.8/
$ ./configure –with-command-group=nagcmd
```

> On Red Hat, the ./configure command might not work and might hang while displaying the message. So, add -enable-redhat-pthread-workaround to the ./configure command as a workaround for the preceding problem, as follows:
>
> ```
> $ make all; sudo make install; sudo make install-init
> $ sudo make install-config; sudo make install-commandmode
> ```

Web interface configuration

- After installing Nagios, we need to do a minimal level of configuration. Explore the /usr/local/nagios/etc directory for a few samples.

- Update /usr/local/nagios/etc/objects/contacts.cfg, with the e-mail address on which you want to receive the alerts.

- Secondly, we need to configure the web interface through which we will monitor and manage the services. Install the Nagios web configuration file in the Apache configuration directory using the following command:

   ```
   $ sudo make install-webconf
   ```

- The preceding command will work only in the extracted directory of the Nagios. Make sure that you have extracted Nagios from the TAR file and are in that directory.

Introduction to Monitoring

- Create an `nagadm` account for logging into the Nagios web interface using the following command:

    ```
    $ sudo htpasswd -c /usr/local/nagios/etc/htpasswd.users nagadm
    ```

- Reload apache, to read the changes, using the following command:

    ```
    $ sudo service httpd restart
    $ sudo /etc/init.d/nagios restart
    ```

- Open `http://localhost/nagios/` in any browser on your machine.

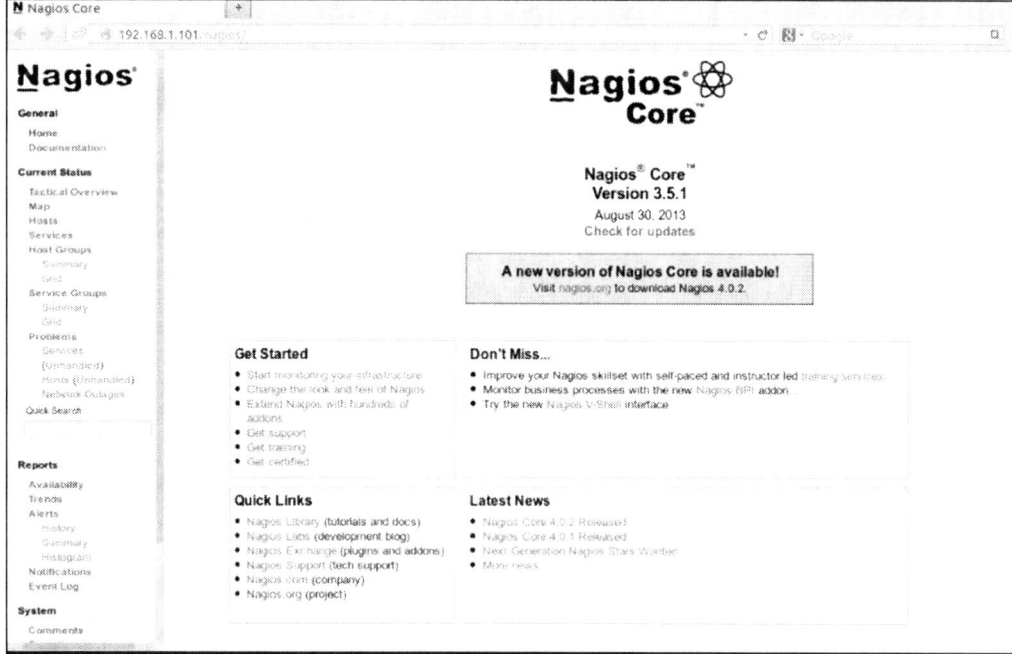

If you see a message, such as **Return code of 127 is out of bounds – plugin may be missing** on the right panel, then this means that your configuration is correct as of now. This message indicates that the Nagios plugins are missing, and we will show you how to install these plugins in the next step.

Nagios plugins

Nagios provides many useful plug-ins to get us started with monitoring all the basics. We can write our custom checks and integrate it with other plug-ins, such as `check_disk`, `check_load`, and many more. Download the latest stable version of the plugins and then extract them. The following command lines help you in extracting and installing Nagios plugins:

```
$ tar zxvf nagios-plugins-2.x.x.tar.gz
$ cd nagios-plugins-2.x.x/
$ ./configure --with-nagios-user=nagios --with-nagios- group=nagios
$ make ; sudo make install
```

After the installation of the core and the plug-in packages, we will be ready to start `nagios`.

Verification

Before starting the Nagios service, make sure that there are no configuration errors by using the following command:

```
$ sudo /usr/local/nagios/bin/nagios -v /usr/local/nagios/etc/nagios.cfg
```

Start the `nagios` service by using the following command:

```
$ sudo service nagios start
$ sudo chkconfig ---add nagios; sudo chkconfig nagios on
```

Configuration files

There are many configuration files in Nagios, but the major ones are located under the `/usr/local/nagios/etc` directory:

Configuration File	Description
nagios.cfg	This controls the `nagios` behavior and contains the global directives.
cgi.cfg	This is the user interface configuration file.
resource.cfg	To safeguard any sensitive information, such as passwords, this file has been made in such a way that it is readable only by the `nagios` user.

Introduction to Monitoring

The other configuration files under the `/usr/local/nagios/etc/objects` directory are described as follows:

Configuration File	Description
`contacts.cfg`	This contains a list of the users who need to be notified by the alerts.
`commands.cfg`	All the commands to check the services are defined here. Use Macros for command substitution.
`localhost.cfg`	This is a baseline file to define the other hosts whom you would like to monitor.

The `nagios.conf` file under `/usr/local/nagios/etc/` is the main configuration file with various directives that define what all the files include. For example, `cfg_dir=<directory_name>`.

Nagios will recursively process all the configuration files in the subdirectories of the directory that you specify with this directive as follows:

```
cfg_dir=/usr/local/nagios/etc/commands
cfg_dir=/usr/local/nagios/etc/services
cfg_dir=/usr/local/nagios/etc/hosts
```

Setting up monitoring for clients

The Nagios server can do an active or a passive check. If the Nagios server proactively initiates a check, then it is an active check. Otherwise, it is a passive check.

The following are the steps for setting up monitoring for clients:

1. Download NRPE addon from `http://www.nagios.org` and then install `check_nrpe`.
2. Create a host and a service definition for the host to be monitored by creating a new configuration file, `/usr/local/nagios/etc/objects/clusterhosts.cfg` for that particular group of nodes.

Chapter 1

Configuring a disk check
```
define host {

    use linux-server
    host_name remotehost
    alias Remote
    Host address 192.168.0.1
    contact_groups admins
}
Service definition sample:

define service {

    use generic-service
    service_description Root Partition
    contact_groups admins
    check_command check_nrpe!check_disk
}
```

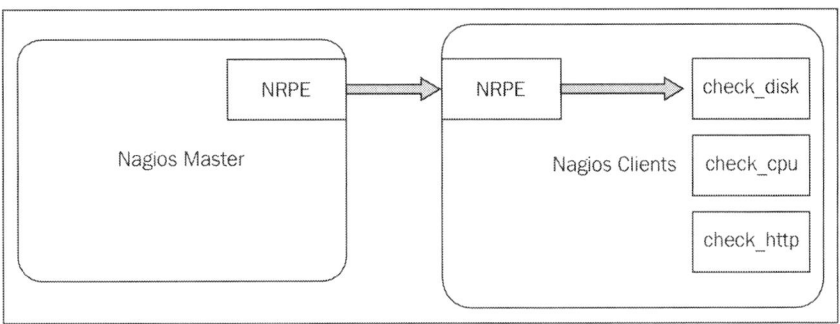

[9]

Introduction to Monitoring

Communication among NRPE components:

- The NRPE on the server (`check_nrpe`) executes the check on the remote NRPE
- The check is returned to the Nagios server through the NRPE on the remote host

On each of the client hosts, perform the following steps:

1. Install the Nagios Plugins and the NRPE addon, as explained earlier.
2. Create an account to run `nagios` from, which can be under any username.

   `[client] # useradd nagios; passwd nagios`

3. Install `nagios-plugin` with the LD flags:

   `[client] # tar xvfz nagios-plugins-2.x.x.tar.gz; cd nagios-plugins-2.x.x/`

   `[client]# export LDFLAGS=-ldl`

   `[client]# ./configure –with-nagios-user=nagios –with- nagios-group=nagios –enable-redhat-pthread-workaround`

   `[client]# make; make install`

4. Change the ownership of the directories, where `nagios` was installed by the `nagios` user:

   `[client]# chown nagios.nagios /usr/local/nagios`

   `[client]# chown -R nagios.nagios /usr/local/nagios/libexec/`

5. Install NRPE and run it as daemon:

   `[client]# tar xvfz nrpe-2.x.tar.gz; cd nrpe-2.x`

   `[client]# ./configure; make all ;make install-plugin; make install-daemon; make install-daemon-config; make install-xinetd`

6. Start the service, after creating the `/et/xinet.d/nrpe` file with the IP of the server:

   `[client#] service xinetd restart`

7. Modify the `/usr/local/nagios/etc/nrpe.cfg` configuration file:
   ```
   command[check_disk]=/usr/local/nagios/libexec/check_disk -w 20% -c 10% -p /dev/hda1
   ```

After getting a good insight into Nagios, we are ready to understand its deployment in the Hadoop clusters.

The second tool that we will look into is Ganglia. It is a beautiful tool for aggregating stats and plotting them nicely. Nagios gives the events and alerts, Ganglia aggregates and presents them in a meaningful way. *What if you want to look for the total CPU, memory per cluster of 2000 nodes or total free disk space on 1000 nodes?* Plotting the CPU memory for one node is easy, but aggregating it for a group on a node requires a tool that can do this.

Ganglia

Ganglia is an open source, distributed monitoring platform for collecting metrics across the cluster. It can do aggregation on CPU, memory, disk I/O, and many more components across a group of nodes. There are alternate tools, such as Cacti and Munin, but Ganglia scales very well for large enterprises.

Some of the key features of Ganglia are as follows:

- You can view historical and real time metrics of a single node or for an entire cluster
- You can use the data to make decisions on the cluster sizing and the performance

Ganglia components

We will now discuss some components of Ganglia.

- **Ganglia Monitoring Daemon** (gmond): It runs on the nodes that need to be monitored, and it captures the state change and sends updates to a central daemon by using XDR.

Introduction to Monitoring

- **Ganglia Meta Daemon** (gmetad): It collects data from gmond and the other gmetad daemons. The data is indexed and stored on the disk in a round robin fashion. There is also a Ganglia front-end for a meaningful display of the information collected.

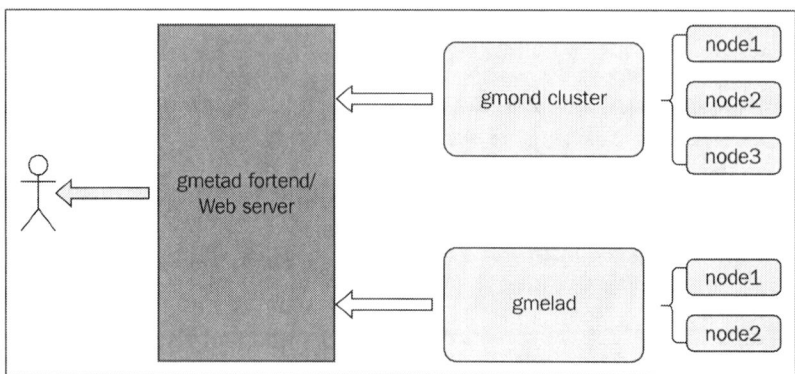

Ganglia installation

Let's begin by setting up Ganglia, and see what the important parameters that need to be taken care of are. Ganglia can be downloaded from http://ganglia.sourceforge.net/. Perform the following steps to install Ganglia:

1. Install gmond on the nodes that need to be monitored:

   ```
   $ sudo apt-get install ganglia-monitor
   Configure /etc/ganglia/gmond.conf
   globals {
     daemonize = yes
     setuid = yes
     user = ganglia
     debug_level = 0
     max_udp_msg_len = 1472
     mute = no
     deaf = no
     host_dmax = 0
     cleanup_threshold = 600
     gexec = no
   send_metadata_interval = 0
   ```

[12]

Chapter 1

```
}
udp_send_channel {
  host = gmetad.cluster1.com
  port = 8649
}
udp_recv_channel {
 port = 8649
}
tcp_accept_channel {
  port = 8649
}
```

2. Restart the Ganglia service:

   ```
   $ service ganglia-monitor restart
   ```

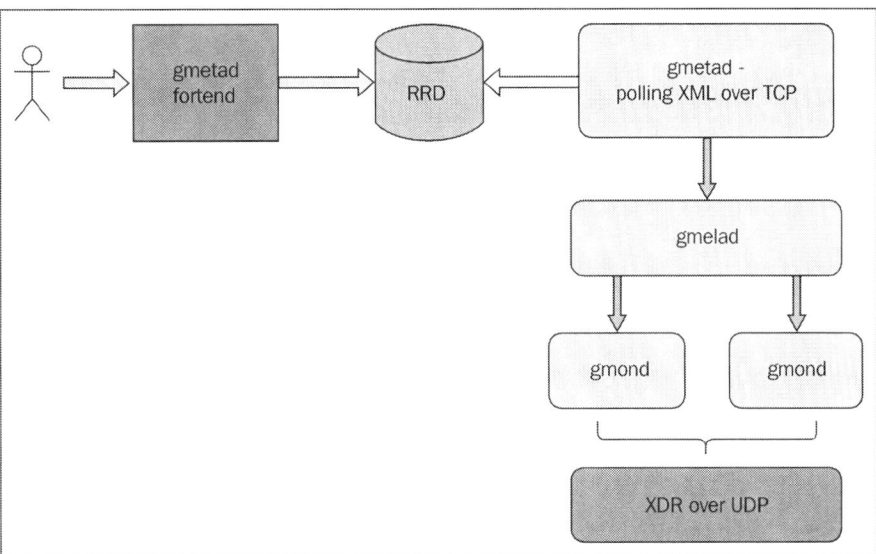

3. Install gmetad on the master node. It can be downloaded from http://ganglia.sourceforge.net/:

   ```
   $ sudo apt-get install gmetad
   ```

4. Update the gmetad.conf file, which tells you where it will collect the data from along with the data source:

   ```
   vi /etc/ganglia/gmetad.conf
   data_source "my cluster" 120 localhost
   ```

5. Update the gmond.conf file on all the nodes so that they point to the master node, which has the same cluster name.

System logging

Logging is an important part of any application or a system, as it tells you about the progress, errors, states of services, security breaches, and repeated user failures, and this helps you in troubleshooting and analyzing these events. The important features about logs are collecting, transporting, storing, alerting, and analyzing the events.

Collection

Logs can be generated in many ways. They can be generated either through system facilities, such as syslog or through applications that can directly write their logs. In either case, the collection of the logs must be organized so that they can be easily retrieved when needed.

Transportation

The logs can be transferred from multiple nodes to a central location, so that instead of parsing logs on hundreds of servers individually, you can maintain them in an easy way by central logging. The size of the logs transferred across the network, and how often we need to transfer them, are also matters of concern.

Storage

The storage needs will depend upon the retention policy of the logs, and the cost will also vary according to the storage media or the location of storage, such as cloud storage or local storage.

Alerting and analysis

The logs collected need to be parsed and the alerts should be sent for any errors. The errors need to be detected in a speculated time frame and remediation should be provided.

Analyzing the logs to identify the traffic patterns of a website is important. The apache web server hosting a website and its logs needs to be analyzed, which IPs were visited, using which user agent or operating system. All of this information can be used to target advertisements at various sections of the internet user base.

The syslogd and rsyslogd daemons

The logging into the Linux system is controlled by the `syslogd` daemons and recently by `rsyslogd` daemons. There is one more logger called `klogd`, which logs kernel messages.

The `syslogd` is configured by `/etc/syslogd.conf` and the format of the file is defined as `facility.priority log_location`.

The logging facility and priority is described in the tables as follows:

Facility	Description
authpriv	These are the security / authorization messages.
cron	These are the clock daemons (`atd` and `crond`).
kern	These are the kernel messages.
local[0-7]	These are reserved for local use.
mail	This is the e-mail system.

The table shown here describes the priority:

Priority	Description
debug	This displays the debugging information.
info	This displays the general informative messages.
warning	This displays the warning messages.
err	This displays an error condition.
crit	This displays the critical condition.
alert	This displays an immediate action that is required.
emerg	This displays that the system is no longer available.

For example, the logging events for an e-mail event can be configured as follows:

`mail.* /var/log/mail`

This command logs all the e-mail messages to the `/var/log/messages` file.

Introduction to Monitoring

Here's another example; start the logging daemon and it will start capturing the logs from the various daemons and applications. Use the following command to perform this action:

```
$ service syslogd/rsyslog restart
```

 In the versions released after RHEL 5 or Centos 5, `syslog` has been replaced by `rsyslogd`.

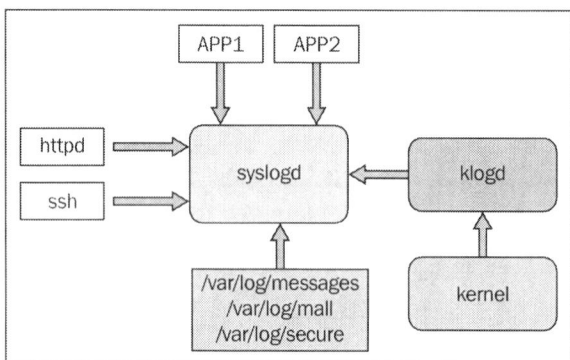

Summary

This chapter has built the base for monitoring, logging, and log collection. In this chapter, we talked about the monitoring concepts, and how we can setup Nagios and Ganglia for monitoring. We also discussed how the structure of the configuration files is, and how they can be segregated into various sections for the ease of use.

Using this as a baseline, we will move on to understand the Hadoop services, the ports used by Hadoop, and then configure monitoring for them in the upcoming chapters of this book.

In the next chapter, we will deal with the Hadoop daemons and services.

2
Hadoop Daemons and Services

In this chapter, we'll look at Hadoop services and try to understand how and on what ports they communicate. The aim of this chapter is not to configure the Hadoop cluster, but to understand it from the perspective of monitoring. Hadoop is a distributed platform with various services running across the cluster. The coordination between services and the way they communicate plays a very important role in the working of the cluster. The communication can be done using TCP/IP or RPC over TCP, or it could be simply done using HTTP.

In this chapter, we will look at the communication between Hadoop components.

The following topics will be covered in this chapter:

- Important services, ports used by Hadoop and how they communicate
- Common issues faced by various daemons
- Host level checks

Hadoop is highly configurable, and we can configure it to work optimally. Each of the Hadoop components has configuration files with which we can control service ports, data directories, and performance parameters.

Hadoop daemons

Hadoop is a distributed framework with two important components: HDFS and MapReduce. Hadoop has two main versions: Hadoop 1.0 and Hadoop 2.0. The original Hadoop 1.0 has NameNode, DataNode, JobTracker, and TaskTracker. In Hadoop 2.0, a new YARN framework has come into picture, which replaces JobTracker and TaskTracker with ResourceManager and NodeManager respectively. HDFS is the File System or the storage layer, and MapReduce is the programming model.

Each layer has a master and a slave to handle the communication and coordination between them. In order to set up monitoring, it is important to take into account the services and ports used by each node.

NameNode

NameNode is the master node that takes care of the HDFS File System. There are many important things to take care in NameNode in terms of services and ports. The following table lists parameters which need to be monitored:

Parameter	Description
dfs.name.dir dfs.namenode.name.dir	This is the parameter in hdfs-site.xml and defines the location of NameNode metadata store. This location must be monitored for disk usage and disk failures, if any.
fs.default.name or fs.defaultFS	This parameter defines the hostname and port on which the NameNode will listen. By default, it is 8020. This is important to monitor in order to maintain the state of NameNode.
dfs.http.address	This is the WebUI port for the NameNode. This port is important for any kind of HTTP communication, such as between secondary and primary NameNode.
dfs.namenode.handler.count	This parameter controls the number of NameNode handler count. By default it is set to 10; you need to monitor the logs to adjust the value accordingly.

It is very important to monitor the key aspects of NameNode to ensure a smooth running cluster. Other important things to keep track of are:

- The NameNode boot up time
- Heap size configuration and its usage
- Disk I/O statistics and performance

DataNode and TaskTracker

DataNode is the slave node of the HDFS layer that stores the actual data. DataNode can have many disks for data storage, which need to be monitored for failures or could impact the I/O performance. Hadoop is designed keeping in mind that some DataNodes will fail. But, it is important to measure and keep track of what percentage of the nodes are up to better plan and utilize the cluster. Some of the important parameters to keep track of this, through monitoring and logs are listed here:

Parameter	Description
dfs.data.dir dfs.datanode.data.dir	This is the parameter in hdfs-site.xml on the DataNode and defines the location of actual data. This location must be monitored for disk usage and disk failures, if any.
dfs.datanode.http.address	This is the WebUI port for the DataNode. This port is important for any HTTP Communication and other Rest API calls.
dfs.datanode.address	This is the DataNode communication port, 50010.
dfs.datanode.ipc.address	This is the DataNode IPC Port, 50020.
dfs.datanode.handler.count	This parameter controls the number of DataNode handler count. By default it is set to 3; you need to monitor the logs to adjust the value accordingly.
tasktracker.http.threads	This parameter controls the threads for the TaskTracker. This can be increased to adjust for the load on the TaskTracker.
mapred.child.java.opts	This parameter controls the memory for the child JVMs. It needs to be adjusted according to the total memory on the system and the number of slots.

TaskTracker runs on DataNode and needs to be monitored for the memory, the temporary space they consume.

Secondary NameNode

Secondary NameNode is critical in the production environment as it performs check pointing. It is important to make sure that the checkpoints happen and the data is consistent. Monitoring must be in place for secondary NameNode to detect any misconfigurations or other errors as soon as possible in order to ensure that if need arises, we can restore the metadata from this node.

Parameter	Description
`dfs.namenode.checkpoint.period`	How often the secondary NameNode should do the check pointing; the default is `3600` seconds.
`dfs.secondary.http.address`	This is the port where the secondary NameNode listens; the default is `50090`. A Rest API call is done using web servers on both the primary and secondary NameNode for the check pointing.
`fs.checkpoint.dir`	This parameter defines the checkpoint directory, where the secondary NameNode will write the metadata. The disk must be monitored for space.
`fs.checkpoint.edits.dir`	This is the directory for pulling the edits from the primary NameNode and writing it here. The disk must be monitored for space.

JobTracker and YARN daemons

The master handles the job submitted to the Hadoop cluster; it could either be JobTracker or ResourceManager, depending upon the Hadoop version. The master needs to take care of the coordination with the slave daemons like TaskTracker for scheduling, resource management, failures, and so on. It is important to keep an eye on the usage and working of these daemons to ensure that the MapReduce layer is healthy. The following table describes the parameters that need to be monitored for this:

Parameter	Description
`mapred.job.tracker.handler.count`	This is the number of threads that the JobTracker runs to handle the requests.
`yarn.resourcemanager.address`	This is the port for the WebUI of the JobTracker; the default is `50030`
`yarn.resourcemanager.scheduler.address`	This is the port for ResourceManager; the default is `8032`.
`yarn.resourcemanager.webapp.address`	This is the port for ResourceManager scheduler; the default is `8030`.

Parameter	Description
`yarn.nodemanager.address`	This is the ResourceManager WebUI port; the default is `8088`. `${yarn.nodemanager.hostname}:0`
`yarn.nodemanager.container-manager.thread-count`	This tells you about the number of threads; the default is `20`.

In addition to all the parameters listed in the preceding table, it is important to configure monitoring for the hosts on which each of these services run. There is no point in keeping the services healthy if the underlying hardware fails or runs out of resources. We will look at the important monitoring checks to do at the host level at a later stage in the chapter.

The communication between daemons

There are lots of ports used in Hadoop; some are for internal communication, such as for scheduling jobs and replication, while others are for user interactions. They may be exposed using TCP or HTTP. Hadoop daemons provide information over HTTP about logs, stacks, and metrics that could be used for troubleshooting. NameNode can expose information about the File System and live or dead nodes, or it can block reports by DataNode or JobTracker to track the running jobs.

Hadoop uses TCP, HTTP, IPC, or Socket for communication among the nodes or daemons. Some of the important communication channels are captured in the following table:

Protocol	Description
HTTP	The communication between primary and secondary NameNode takes over HTTP. Also, the transfer between mappers and reducers is done over HTTP. In addition to this, there are a lot of Rest APIs exposed for File System operations using WebHDFS and others.
Raw sockets	This is used for copying data across DataNodes like replication and others.
RPC over TCP	This is used for communication between NameNode and DataNodes.
Other APIs	For example: Connecting to RM from client uses a protocol implemented using the (AsM) Application Manager interface. HDFS also provides APIs to the client to talk to it. This can be a simple `java.io`.

The client can talk to the NameNode using ClientProtocol. The connection is established over TCP by using the RPC call. Using this protocol, the client can create, delete, append, or add block.

- The channel between DataNode and client is a streaming channel and not RPC due to performance concerns. The data transfer from the client is sent directly to the DataNodes.
- DataNode always initiates the communication between NameNode and DataNode; keep in mind that NameNode never initiates a connection. The DataNode can register, de-register, and send block reports and heartbeat at defined intervals. This is depicted in the the following diagram:

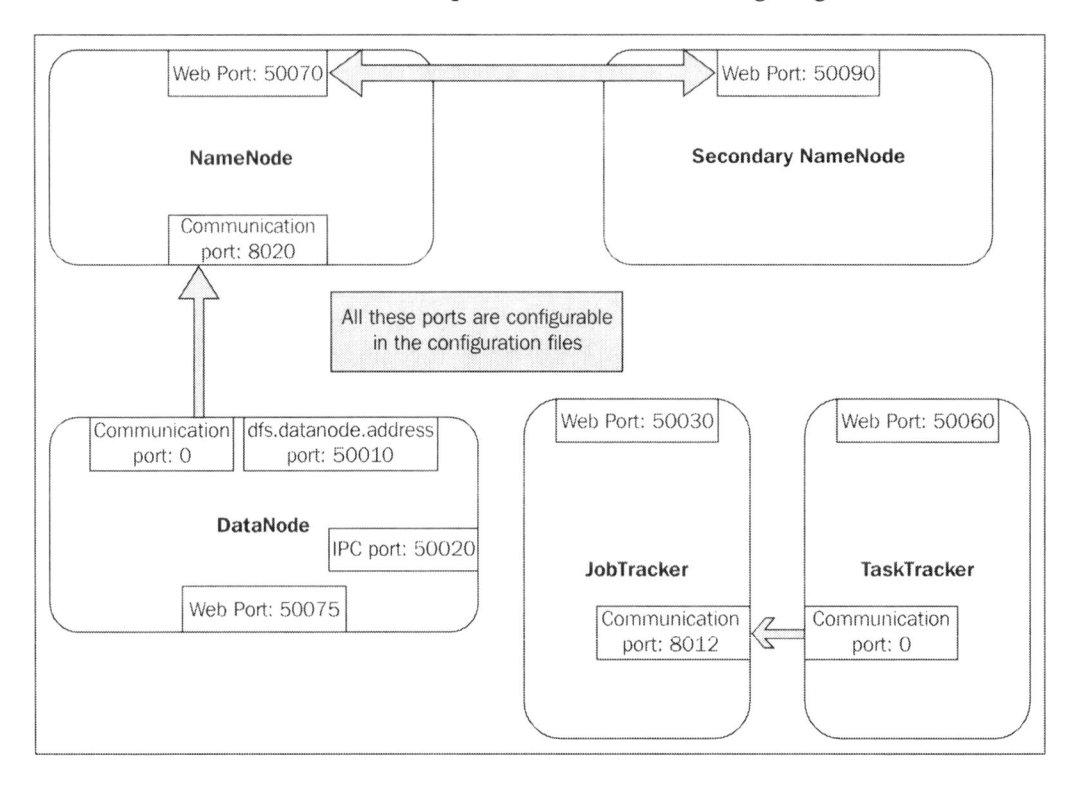

YARN framework

The **YARN** (**Yet Another Resource Negotiator**) is the new MapReduce framework. It is designed to scale for large clusters and performs much better as compared to the old framework. There are new sets of daemons in the new framework, and it is good to understand how they communicate with each other. The following diagram explains the daemons and ports on which they talk:

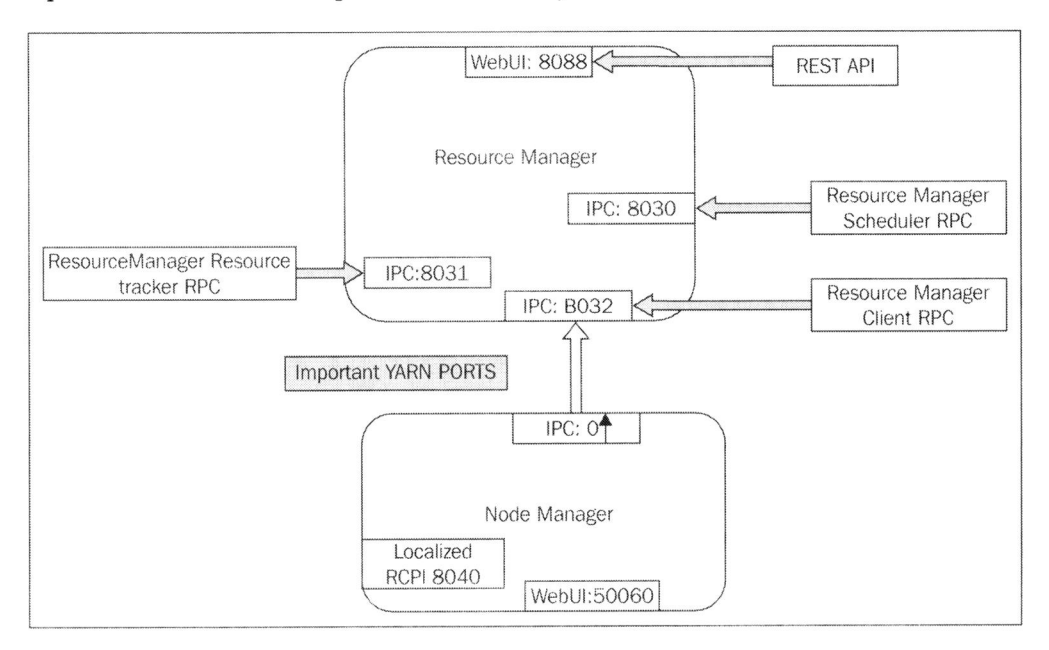

Common issues faced on Hadoop cluster

With a distributed framework of the scale of Hadoop, many things can go wrong. It is not possible to capture all the issues that could occur, but from a monitoring perspective, we can list the things that are common and can be monitored easily. The following table tries to capture the common issues faced in Hadoop:

Issue	Description and steps that could help
High CPU utilization	This could be due to high query rate or faulty job. Use `top` command to find the offending processes. On NameNode, it could be due to a large number of handlers or DataNodes sending block reports at the same time. Explore the `initDelay` parameter.
High memory utilization	This is a misconfiguration of `HEAP_SIZE`; more MapReduce tasks are configured to run with large memory setting. It's running non-Hadoop jobs on the nodes.
Disk space utilization	If you do not have a right retention policy in place and have unnecessary data, the solution is to delete scratch spaces and add DataNodes or more disks per node.
Data block corruptions	These are node failures and disk failures. Make sure you have the `replication` set to at least 3.
NameNode metadata directory location alerts.	Make sure all the edits' locations are accessible to the NameNode. Check for permissions or reachability if it's over NFS.
Process down	The daemons could be down due to crash; make sure all the daemons are up and responding to health checks.
NameNode response time	Too many operations are being performed by NameNode, network load, faulty NIC or other hardware components.
Cluster low on total storage	The number of live DataNodes in the cluster might have gone down.
Slow on read/write	This could be due to wrong settings on HDFS and other buffer parameters. Make sure you do benchmarking, before using the cluster in production.
Network congestion	In addition to the issues local to the node, there can be network issues like congestion on devices due to high traffic or a faulty **NIC (Network Interface Card)**.
Speed of network devices	As in Hadoop, we deal with a large amount of data, so it's important to make sure the devices that carry data can handle jumbo frames and withstand high throughput.

All the checks mentioned in the preceding table and the way nodes communicate will help us in setting the monitoring in the right manner. In the upcoming chapters, we'll look at the process of configuring alerts for the parameters mentioned in the preceding table.

Host-level checks

Irrespective of how well the Hadoop daemons are configured and optimized, the underlying hardware is critical for proper functioning of the cluster. There are some standard checks in Nagios, which must be configured on every host in the cluster. Let's look at the host level checks in Nagios and how we will configure them, which is shown in the following diagram:

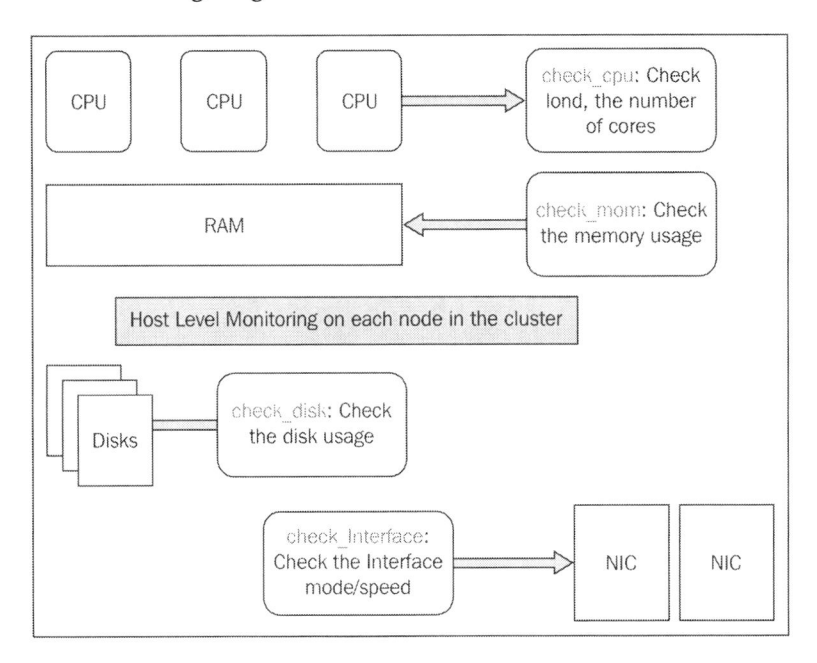

Nagios server

As discussed in the *Chapter 1, Introduction to Monitoring*, this is the master of the Nagios monitoring system and will contain the main configuration files for each service. Firstly, we define checks for each service. Create a `services.conf` file at the base of the Nagios server with the following configuration:

Service SSH:

```
define service {
  hostgroup_name hadoop
  service_description SSH
  check_command check_ssh
  use generic-service
  notification_interval 0
}
```

Service Disk Space:

```
define service {
  hostgroup_name hadoop
  service_description Disk
  check_command check_disk
  use generic-service
  notification_interval 0
}
```

Service Processes:

```
define service {
  hostgroup_name hadoops
  service_description Processes
  check_command check_procs
  use generic-service
  notification_interval 0
}
```

Service Load:

```
define service {
  hostgroup_name hadoop
  service_description Load
  check_command check_load
  use generic-service
  notification_interval 0
}
```

Similarly, we can add this for all the checks we need for a host. Now, we need to configure remote execution for each of the above services using the following script:

```
define service {
  hostgroup_name generic-servers
  service_description Current Load
  check_command check_nrpe_1arg!check_load
  use generic-service
  notification_interval 0
}
```

And host definition for each host is shown in the following code:

```
define host {
  host_name dn1
  alias dn1.cluster1.com
  hostgroups general-servers
  address dn1.cluster1.com
  use generic-host
}
```

Please refer to *Chapter 1, Introduction to Monitoring*, for details of the preceding sections.

Configuring Hadoop nodes for monitoring

On the nodes running Hadoop, we need to put the checks for the respective services along with the libraries. After the installation of the NRPE plugins on each of the hosts, there will be a configuration file `/usr/local/nagios/etc/nrpe.conf`, which actually executes the checks on being invoked by the server, as shown in the following script:

```
command[check_users]=/usr/lib/nagios/plugins/check_users -w 5 -c 10
command[check_load]=/usr/lib/nagios/plugins/check_load -w 15,10,5 -c 30,25,20
command[check_all_disks]=/usr/lib/nagios/plugins/check_disk -w 20% -c 10%
command[check_zombie_procs]=/usr/lib/nagios/plugins/check_procs -w 5 -c 10 -s Z
command[check_total_procs]=/usr/lib/nagios/plugins/check_procs -w 150 -c 200
command[check_swap]=/usr/lib/nagios/plugins/check_swap -w 50% -c 25%
```

Hadoop Daemons and Services

After restarting the Nagios service, hit `http://nagiosserver`, we will start seeing the graphs as shown in the following screenshot. The following screenshot displays the generic checks per host:

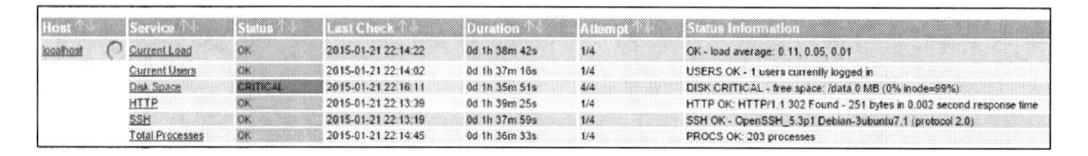

Similarly, for CPU load, the graph will be as shown in the following screenshot:

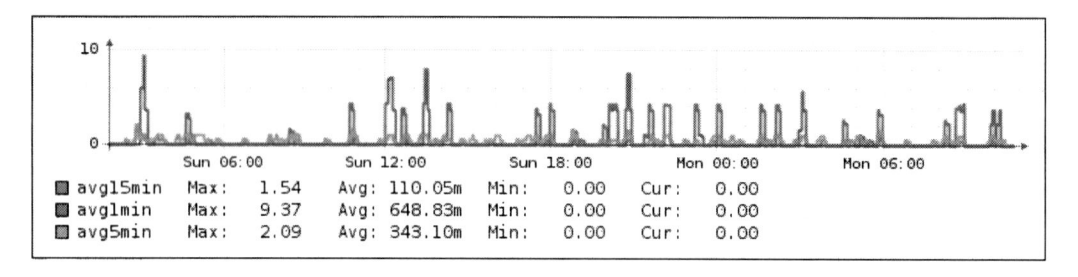

Summary

In this chapter, we discussed important Hadoop daemons and the ports on which they listen. Each daemon listens on a specific port and communicates with the respective daemons using a specific protocol. We looked at the ports for NameNode, DataNodes, and JobTracker and how they talk to each other.

Then we set up monitoring for each of the Hadoop nodes to enable host level checks such as disk quota, CPU usage, memory usage, and so on. In the upcoming chapters, we will talk about configuring checks for Hadoop services. In the next chapter, we will deal with Hadoop logging.

3
Hadoop Logging

In any enterprise, how ever big or small it could be, logging is very important for security and improvement of services. With more and more systems going online, not just logging data but also reviewing the logs is very important.

Systems today are generating millions of lines of data, which could be simple web events, some database query logs, network logs, or any audit logs. Dealing with such large logs manually is neither practical nor viable in terms of time; there must be centralized logging and analysis tools to quickly extract the useful information.

In this chapter, we begin our journey by exploring the concepts of logging at both the system level and Hadoop level.

We'll cover the following topics in this chapter:

- Different log levels
- Logs written by various Hadoop daemons
- Understanding audit logs and how they could be useful

The need for logging events

The events can be generated by system daemons, applications, or other services running on it. To keep a track of the functionality, errors, performance and security, it is important to capture events and analyze them to find the cause of failure and/or intrusion. Logging is done for:

- **Accountability**: On any system there are multiple users and what they do must be tracked, and if needed, the events should be linked to user accounts for accountability.
- **Intrusion detection**: Any unusual or unauthorized activity can be traced using logs. Unusual login attempts, access from suspicious IPs, modification of system binaries, installation of backdoors, and so on can be tracked using logs.
- **Problem detection**: Application failures and resource constraints, such as out of memory errors, write events into logs, which can help in narrowing down the issue.

The logs provide a proactive approach in terms of finding any security holes and help in plugging them on time. By collecting and analyzing logs, we can understand what goes within the infrastructure. Each log contains important information about a service or a user, which can be used to analyze important events and helps in troubleshooting issues.

The data generated by log collection could be huge, so it is important to understand what to log. The intent should be to log important things, but sometimes identifying what is important is a challenge. Let's start with understanding logging system at the system level and then move on to Hadoop.

System logging

In Linux, the daemon responsible for logging is `syslogd` or recently the newer version `rsyslogd`. Applications or daemons write various logs in different files under `/var/log` using `syslogd` daemon, which is controlled by the `syslog.conf` configuration file. The logs can be collected on independent nodes or at a central location using Apache Flume and can be analyzed by using tools such as Flume, Splunk, Logstash, and so on.

There are different logging levels according to how the verbosity of the information logged into files is decided. Each application calls `syslog()` using an internal function, the `log_level`, and writes events to appropriate files.

Logging levels

Every rule consists of two fields—selector field and action field. The selector field specifies a pattern of facilities and priority. Facility and priority is separated by a .; facility specifies the subsystem that produced the message. Table 1 lists out facilities and Table 2 lists out priorities:

Table 1: Facility

Facility	Description
Kernel	Kernel messages
User	User level messages
Mail	Mail messages
Daemon	System messages
FTP	FTP server messages

The log severity can be controlled using the `priority` option, and we can make it as verbose as we like. The trade off is always between size of logs and what to log.

Table 2: Priorities

Severity	Description
0	Emergency, system unstable
1	Alert: Immediate action
2	Critical: The state of the system/application is critical
3	Error condition: The system is throwing errors
4	Warning
7	Debug. Verbose logging of information

Log kernel-related messages to a separate file, with the pattern as kernel subsystem and all priority, to be logged to a file, as shown here:

`Kern.* /var/log/kern.log`

Logs related to mail messages, as shown here:

`Mail.* /var/log/maillog`

The syslog architecture is very robust and well-designed. The protocol provides a transportation to allow a device to send notifications across networks to event collectors. The syslog message size is limited to 1024 bytes and carries information such as facility, severity, and timestamp. The following diagram depicts the Syslog Architecture, which can feed to other distributed log management systems:

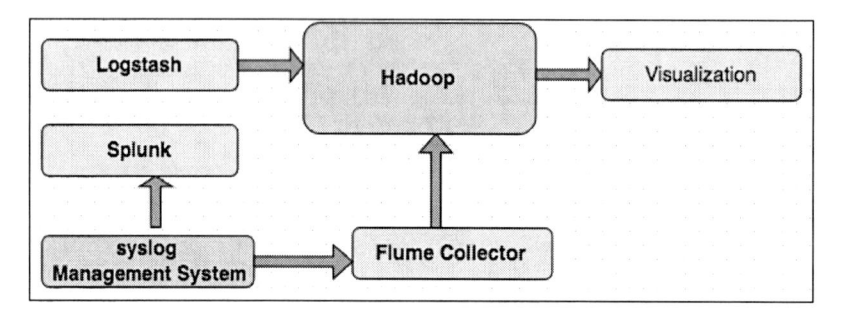

Logging in Hadoop

In Hadoop, each daemon writes its own logs and the severity of logging is configurable. The logs in Hadoop can be related to the daemons or the jobs submitted. They are useful to troubleshoot slowness, issues with MapReduce tasks, connectivity issues, and platform bugs. The logs generated can be user level like task tracker logs on each node or can be related to master daemons such as NameNode and JobTracker.

In the newer YARN platform, there is a feature to move the logs to HDFS after initial logging. In Hadoop 1.x, the user log management is done using UserLogManager, which cleans and truncates logs according to retention and size parameters such as `mapred.userlog.retain.hours` and `mapreduce.cluster.map.userlog.retain-size` respectively. The tasks standard out and error are piped to the Unix tail program, so it retains the required size only.

These are some of the challenges of log management in Hadoop:

- **Excessive logging**: The truncation of logs is not done till the tasks finish; this is because many jobs could cause disk space issues as the amount of data written is quite large.
- **Truncation**: We can't always say what to log and how much is good enough. For some users, 500 KB of logs might be good, but for some 10 MB might not suffice.

- **Retention**: How long you need to retain logs: one month or six months? There is no standard rule, but there are best practices or governance issues for retention. In many countries, there is regulation in place to keep data for one year. The best practice for any organization is to keep it for at least six months.
- **Analysis**: What should be done if we want to look at historical data, how to aggregate logs onto a central system, and do analyses? In Hadoop, logs are served, by default, over HTTP for a single node.

Some of the preceding issues have been addressed in the YARN framework. Rather then truncating logs specially on individual nodes, the logs can be moved to HDFS and processed using other tools. The logs are written at the per application level into directories per application. The user can access these logs through the command line or web UI. For example, $HADOOP_YARN_HOME/bin/yarn logs.

Hadoop logs

In addition to the logs generated by each daemon whether they're NameNode, DataNode, JobTracker, or secondary NameNode, there are other logs such as configuration logs, statistic, and error logs. In Hadoop, the logs can be classified into the following categories:

- **Hadoop daemon logs**: These are the logs related to the Hadoop daemons, and there will be one log file for each daemon on a host. If we are run a pseudo mode of Hadoop, which means running NameNode, JobTracker, DataNode, TaskTracker, and secondary NameNode all on the same node, there will be five log files for each with extension .log.
- **Logging format**: hadoop-$(user-running-hadoop)-$(daemon)-hostname.log.
- **Job logs**: There are two type of job logs in Hadoop; one is the job configuration log for each job submitted to JobTracker and the other is the statistics log for the tasks attempts, shuffle, and so on. The JobTracker creates an XML file for each job, which will be stored at the $HADOOP_HOME/log location. The naming convention for these jobs is job_<jobid>_config.xml.
- **Log4j**: The jobs have many sub parts called tasks, and their logs are written by log4j. It provides an interface to the developer to hook map and reduce jobs to logs. These logs can be very intensive, depending upon the number of calls done to the logging system.
- **Error logs**: The TaskTracker writes errors to standard out and standard error of any task attempts.

There are many variables which control logging for the daemons in Hadoop. The following table captures some of these variables:

Table 3:

Parameter	Description
HADOOP_LOG_DIR	This is defined in the file hadoop-env.sh and it defines the location where the logs are written.
mapreduce.jobtracker.jobhistory.location	This stores the job history and by default it is ${hadoop.log.dir}/history. It is defined in the mapred-site.xml file.
mapreduce.map.log.level	This is the logging level for map tasks, such as INFO, ERROR, OFF, DEBUG, and ALL. It is defined in mapred-site.xml.
mapreduce.reduce.log.level	This is the logging level for MapReduce tasks such as INFO, ERROR, OFF, DEBUG, and ALL. It is defined in mapred-site.xml.
mapreduce.task.userlog.limit.kb	This is the size of the task logs and it is defined in mapred-site.xml.
yarn.app.mapreduce.am.container.log.limit.kb	This is the size of the MRAppMaster logs.
mapreduce.job.userlog.retain.hours	These are the hours for which the logs must be retained.
dfs.namenode.logging.level	This is the logging level for NameNode. The default is INFO; it is configured in the hdfs-site.xml file.
dfs.namenode.audit.loggers	This is the default Hadoop audit logger.

Hadoop log level

In Hadoop, we can control the verbosity of the information logged into the logs in a similar manner to how we do with the syslog log level. In Hadoop, the log level is defined by the parameter HADOOP_ROOT_LOGGER in hadoop-env.sh.

The default configuration for this looks like the one shown as follows:

```
export HADOOP_ROOT_LOGGER="INFO,CONSOLE"
```

The preceding configuration is specified in the file hadoop-env.sh, and it states that the logging level is INFO and the destination is tied to the console.

This configuration could create a lot of noise as it is logging a lot of information. This can be modified by using the **DRFA (Daily Rolling File Appender)** and by reducing the log level, shown as follows:

`export HADOOP_ROOT_LOGGER="WARN,DRFA"`

DRFA allows the logs to go to a file appender rather then the standard out or error.

Another important configuration file is the `conf/log4j.properties` file, which can also be used to configure logging and auditing in Hadoop. The logging level can be changed as shown here, by configuring it in the file `conf/log4j.properties`:

`hadoop.root.logger=WARN,DRFA`

`hadoop.log.dir=.`

`hadoop.log.file=hadoop.log`

The `hadoop.log` will be in the directory defined by `$HADOOP_LOG_DIR`.

The following diagram shows the Hadoop Logging Architecture:

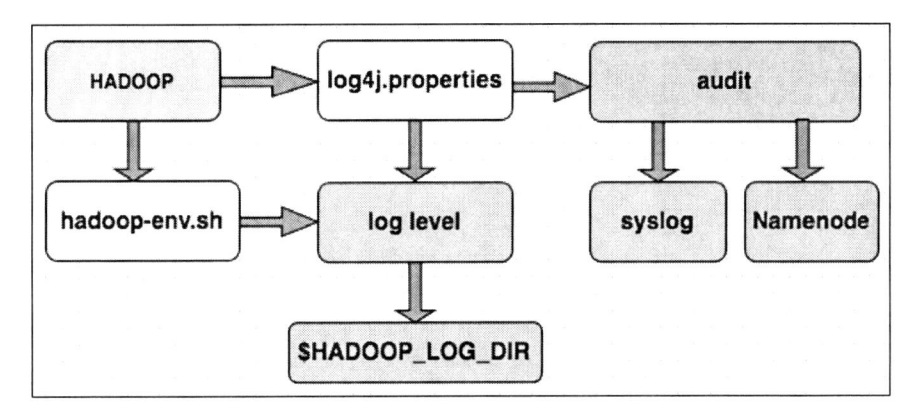

Hadoop audit

We can enable auditing for NameNode and track the user activity such as which user executed what command and who did what. By default, audit logs are sent to NameNode, but this could be overwhelming due to other information written to the logs. We can configure the audit logs to be handled by the `syslog` facility of the Linux system. For this we need to enable `DRFAADUIT`. Similarly, MapReduce and YARN can also be audited and logged with wealth of information such as username, application ID, job queue, duration, and memory allocated.

Log4j.properties:

```
# First disable the audit to be written to namenode:
log4j.additivity.org.apache.hadoop.hdfs.server.namenode.FSNamesystem.audit=false
# Redirect it to the syslog appender:
log4j.logger.org.apache.hadoop.hdfs.server.namenode.FSNamesystem.audit=INFO,DRFAAUDIT,SYSLOG
# Configure local appender:
log4j.appender.DRFAAUDIT=org.apache.log4j.DailyRollingFileAppender
log4j.appender.DRFAAUDIT.File=/var/log/audit.log
log4j.appender.DRFAAUDIT.DatePattern=.yyyy-MM-dd
log4j.appender.DRFAAUDIT.layout=org.apache.log4j.PatternLayout
log4j.appender.DRFAAUDIT.layout.ConversionPattern=%d{ISO8601} %p %c: %m%n

# Configure syslog appender:
log4j.appender.SYSLOG=org.apache.log4j.net.SyslogAppender
log4j.appender.SYSLOG.syslogHost=loghost
log4j.appender.SYSLOG.layout=org.apache.log4j.PatternLayout
log4j.appender.SYSLOG.layout.ConversionPattern=%d{ISO8601} %p %c: %m%n
log4j.appender.SYSLOG.Facility=LOCAL1
```

Summary

In this chapter, you learned about the Hadoop logging process, daemons, jobs write logs and their locations, and how you can control the log level. You also looked at the log4j log appender and how you can enable audit for Hadoop events. In the next chapter, you'll look at the HDFS checks and how to set up Nagios checks for that.

4
HDFS Checks

The Hadoop distributed File System is an important component of the cluster. The state of the File System must be clean at all stages and the components related to it must be healthy.

In this chapter, we will look at the HDFS checks by using the Hadoop commands, and we will also discuss how to set up the Nagios monitoring for them.

The following topics will be covered in this chapter:

- Replication consistency
- Space utilization
- CPU utilization
- NameNode health checks
- Number of DataNodes in a cluster

HDFS overview

HDFS is a distributed File System that has been designed for robustness by having multiple copies of blocks across the File System. The metadata for the File System is stored on NameNode and the actual data blocks are stored on DataNodes. For a healthy File System, the metadata must be consistent, DataNode blocks must be clean, and replication must be consistent. Let's look at each of these one by one and learn how they can be monitored. The protocol used for communication between NameNode and DataNodes is RPC, and the protocol used for data transfer is HDFS over HTTP.

- **HDFS checks**: Hadoop natively provides the commands to verify the File System. The commands must be run by the user, with whom the HDFS is running. This is mostly HDFS, or you can have any other user. But do not run it as root. To run these commands, the PATH variable must be set and it must include the path to the Hadoop binaries.
    - hadoop dfsadmin -report: This command provides an exclusive report of the HDFS state, the number of DataNodes, and the replication state
- hadoop fsck /: This command is similar to the fsck command of the Linux file system. It does checks for bad blocks and it also has options for extensive checks of the files for the block location, replication, and so on. hadoop fsck / -files -blocks -locations
    - hadoop fs -dus and hadoop fs -count -q /: The above commands give the information about disk usage and the quotas for the File System.
    - jps: This command tells us about the daemons running on Nodes, such as NameNode, DataNode, JobTracker, and so on.

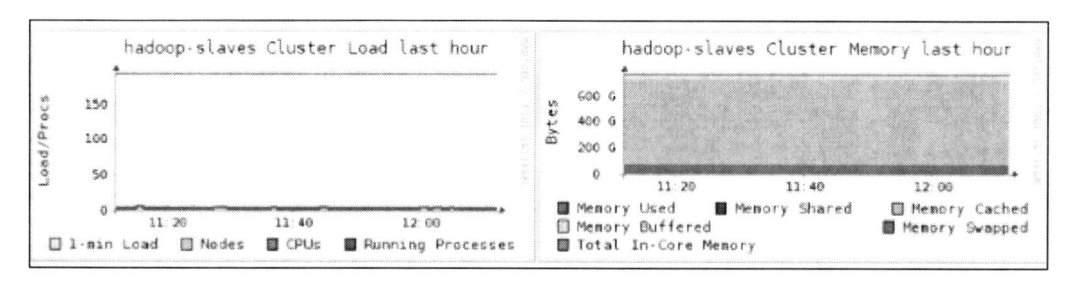

Nagios master configuration

As discussed in *Chapter 1*, *Introduction to Monitoring*, Nagios is a monitoring platform, and it works very well for the Hadoop monitoring needs. Let's see how to configure Nagios for the Hadoop service checks.

On the Nagios server, called `mnode`, we need to set up the service definitions, the command definitions, and the host definitions as defined here. These definitions will enable checks, and by using these we can gather the status of a service or a node. The plugin needs to be downloaded and installed from http://www.nagios.org/download.

- **HDFS space check**: Check the HDFS space usage on the cluster.
  ```
  define command{
    command_name check_hadoop_space
    command_line $PATH$/check_hadoop_namenode.pl -H $HOSTADDRESS$ -u $USER8$ -P $PORT$ -s $ARG2$ -w $ARG3$ -c $ARG4$
  }

  define host {

    use hadoop-server
    host_name hadoopnode1
    alias Remote
    Host address 192.168.0.1
    contact_groups admins
  }
  Service definition:

  define service {

    use generic-service
    service_description space
    contact_groups admins

    check_command check_hadoop_space
  }
  ```

  > For further information, refer to:
  > http://exchange.nagios.org/directory/Plugins/Clustering-and-High-2DAvailability/check_hadoop_namenode-2Epl-%28Advanced-Nagios-Plugins-Collection%29/details

- **Checking the HDFS replication**: Check the HDFS replication on the File System by using the following commands:

  ```
  define command{
    command_name check_replication
    command_line $PATH$/check_hadoop_namenode.pl -H $HOSTADDRESS$ -u $USER8$ -P $PORT$ -r $ARG2$ -w $ARG3$ -c $ARG4$
  }

  define host {

    use hadoop-server
    host_name hadoopnode1
    alias Remote
    Host address 192.168.0.1
    contact_groups admins
  }
  Service definition:

  define service {

    use generic-service
    service_description replication
    contact_groups admins

    check_command check_replication
  }

  Reports under replicated, corrupt replicas, missing blocks
  ```

- **Checking the HDFS balancer**: Check for the balance of the cluster in terms of the usage across different DataNodes. Report the DataNodes that are imbalanced.

  ```
  define command{
    command_name check_balance
    command_line $PATH$/check_hadoop_namenode.pl -H $HOSTADDRESS$ -u $USER8$ -P $PORT$ -b $ARG2$
  }

  define host {

    use hadoop-server
  ```

```
    host_name hadoopnode1
    alias Remote
    Host address 192.168.0.1
    contact_groups admins
}
Service definition:

define service {

  use generic-service
  service_description balance
  contact_groups admins

  check_command check_balance
}
```

- **Counting the HDFS DataNode**: Use the following commands to check for the number of DataNodes against a threshold:

```
define command{
  command_name check_node_count
  command_line $PATH$/check_hadoop_namenode.pl -H $HOSTADDRESS$ -u $USER8$ -P $PORT$ -m $ARG2$ -w $ARG3$ -c $ARG4$
}

define host {

  use hadoop-server
  host_name hadoopnode1
  alias Remote
  Host address 192.168.0.1
  contact_groups admins
}
Service definition:

define service {

  use generic-service
  service_description datanode_count
  contact_groups admins

  check_command check_node_count
}
```

- **Checking the NameNode heap usage**: Use the commands given as follows for checking the heap utilization of the NameNode. The threshold is specified in terms of percentile:

  ```
  define command{
    command_name check_namenode_heap
    command_line $PATH$/check_hadoop_namenode.pl -H $HOSTADDRESS$ -u $USER8$ -P $PORT$ --heap-usage $ARG2$ -w $ARG3$ -c $ARG4$
  }

  define host {

    use hadoop-server
    host_name hadoopnode1
    alias Remote
    Host address 192.168.0.1
    contact_groups admins
  }
  Service definition:

  define service {

    use generic-service
    service_description namenode_heap
    contact_groups admins

    check_command check_namenode_heap
  }
  ```

- **Checking Zookeeper**: The following commands can be used for checking the zookeeper state with the Zookeeper hosts specified in a comma separated list of hosts.

  ```
  define command{
    command_name check_zookeeper
    command_line $PATH$/ check_zookeeper_znode.pl -H $HOSTADDRESS$ -u $USER8$ -P $PORT$ --heap-usage $ARG2$ -w $ARG3$ -c $ARG4$
  }

  define host {

    use hadoop-server
    host_name hadoopnode1
  ```

```
    alias Remote
    Host address 192.168.0.1
    contact_groups admins
}
Service definition:

define service {

  use generic-service
  service_description zookeeper
  contact_groups admins

  check_command check_zookeeper
}
```

The Nagios client configuration

Every Hadoop node, whether NameNode, DataNode, or Zookeeper is a client node of the Nagios Server. Each node must have the NRPE plugin installed with the checks described under `/usr/local/nagios/libexec` and the commands specified under `/usr/local/nagios/etc/nrpe.cfg` as shown here:

`command[check_balancer]=/usr/local/nagios/libexec/check_hadoop_namenode.pl -H $HOSTADDRESS$ -u $USER8$ -P $PORT$ -b $ARG2$`

`command[check_zkp]=/usr/local/nagios/libexec/check_zkpd`

Similarly, entries need to be made for each check that is executed on the nodes.

In addition to the aforementioned plugins, checks must be in place for hardware, disk, CPU, and memory. You should check the number of processes running on a system by using the `check_procs` plugin, check the open ports by using `check_tcp`. Make sure that all the nodes have `ntp` running and that the time is synced by using `check_ntp`. All of these are provided as the standard Nagios system plugins, and they must be placed on each node.

Summary

In this chapter, we looked at how to set up monitoring for the HDFS components, such as the HDFS space utilization, the number of DataNodes in a cluster, heap usage, replication, and the Zookeeper state. In the next chapter, we will look at checks and monitoring for the map reducing components, such as the JobTracker, the TaskTracker, and the various utilization parameters.

5
MapReduce Checks

The Hadoop cluster might have many jobs running on it at any given time, making it extremely important to monitor and make sure that it is running perfectly. The Hadoop clusters are multi-tenant clusters, which mean that multiple users with different use cases and data sizes run jobs on it. How do we make sure that each user or job is getting what it is configured for on the cluster?

In this chapter, we will look at the checks related to MapReduce and its related components. The following topics will be covered in this chapter:

- MapReduce checks
- JobTracker and related health checks
- CPU utilization of MapReduce jobs
- Memory utilization of MapReduce jobs
- YARN component checks
- Total cluster capacity in terms of memory and CPU

MapReduce overview

MapReduce is the programming model designed to leverage the advantages of a distributed framework in a better way. It is a framework that takes care of various phases a job goes through like initialization, submission, execution, and failure recovery. In addition, there are intermediate stages, such as the map, combiner, shuffle, sort, compression, and reducer stage. Each affects the performance of a job or task and must be monitored for the resource utilization at each stage. Both Hadoop version 1 and version 2 can be monitored using Nagios. In YARN, we have ResourceManager, NodeManager, Application Manager, and few other components, all of which can be monitored using Nagios.

Before going to Nagios checks, there are some important commands and logs, which give us a good idea about the current state of the cluster in terms of the MapReduce operations.

> Hadoop natively provides commands to verify the jobs and its related information.

MapReduce control commands

Hadoop provides a job command to interact with map reducers, using which the administrator can control the jobs or tasks submitted to the cluster.

- The `<options>` part of `hadoop job <options>` is explained in the following table:

Option	Description
-list	This command lists all the running jobs in a cluster. This is for MapReduce version 1.
-list all	This command lists all the jobs in a cluster.
-status <job-id>	This gives information about the job counter and the MapReduce completion percentage.
-kill <job-id>	Using this command, we can kill the long-running or stuck jobs.
-history	Gives details about the job, in terms of failed or successful tasks.

- `hadoop jobtracker -dumpConfiguration`: This command is used to dump the JobTracker configuration along with all the queue information. This can be really helpful in doing a quick review of the configuration or as a backup.

- `hadoop queue <options>`: The jobs submitted can be sub-divided or organized into job queues. Each queue is assigned a capacity and the users who could submit jobs to it.

  We can use `-list` to see the list of queues and scheduling information associated with it.

In the new MapReduce version **MRv2**, we have YARN, which controls the jobs submitted to the cluster. It manages the resources in a much better and intelligent way. The commands for the job control in the YARN framework are given as follows:

`yarn application <options>`

The `<options>` part of `yarn application <options>` is explained in the following table:

Option	Description
`-list`	Here, we talk in terms of applications and not jobs, which are controlled by the **RM** (which stands for **Resource Manager**). The beauty of this new command is that we can filter out applications according to type and state.
`-appStates States`	States can be `running`, `Finished`, `ALL`, `Killed`, and so on.
`-status <app-id>`	This gives information about the application.
`-kill <app-id`	Using this command, we can kill the long-running or stuck jobs.

In the new version MRv2, in addition to information about applications (jobs), we can list the nodes, their states, and the application logs as follows:

- `yarn node <options>`: This command lists the nodes, which are up in terms of the communication with the RM. In simple terms, the nodes that are running. The node list can be filtered according to the state of the nodes as well.

- `yarn logs -applicationId <app Id> <options>`: This command spits out logs for the specific application with the option to pull information specific to the owner or the node of execution. The best thing in the new framework is that we do not need to go to the specific node of execution to see the logs. All the logs can be pulled from a central command line interface.

In addition to the above, there are a few administration commands to check the health of the RM and set the log level at each node. The commands that can help to do this are as follows:

- `yarn rmadmin -checkHealth <serviceId>`: This command is used to check the state of RM, whether it is active or standby, and is used in **high availability (HA)**.
- `yarn daemonlog -setlevel <host:port> <name> <level>`: This command is used to set the log level of each daemon on a particular host. This is an easy way to control the log level across different nodes in a cluster.

MapReduce health checks

There are many factors that impact the performance of a job or application submitted to the cluster. The important checks, which can help narrow down the bottlenecks and help in improving the performance, can be many, but the few important ones are as follows:

- Health of JobTracker or the RM
- Backlog of tasks in the cluster; make sure that the number of tasks does not cross the upper limit of the maximum tasks supported in the cluster
- Localities of the tasks run to make sure that there is minimal across-rack traffic
- Health of TaskTracker and other components like NodeManager depending upon the MR version

The above checks are very well-documented and talked about at the Cloudera website. Please read them for further understanding.

Nagios master configuration

As discussed in earlier chapters, Nagios is a monitoring platform and works very well for the Hadoop monitoring needs. Let's see how to configure Nagios for Hadoop service checks.

Chapter 5

On the Nagios server, called mnode, we need to set up service definitions, command definitions, and the host definition. All these plugins are available at the Nagios website and can be downloaded from there.

- **JobTracker health check**: This is used to check the JobTracker status:

```
define command{
  command_name check_jobtracker_health
  command_line $PATH$/check_hadoop_mapreduce_nodes.pl -H $HOSTADDRESS$ -P $PORT$
}

define host {

  use hadoop-server
  host_name jt1
  alias Remote
  Host address 192.168.0.1
  contact_groups admins
}
Service definition:

define service {

  use generic-service
  service_description jobtracker
  contact_groups admins

  check_command check_jobtracker_health
}
```

> For further information, refer to
> http://exchange.nagios.org/directory/Plugins/Clustering-and-High-2DAvailability/check_hadoop_mapreduce_nodes-2Epl-%28Advanced-Nagios-Plugins-Collection%29/details.

[49]

MapReduce Checks

- **Number of alive nodes**: This is used to check the number of nodes that are alive and talking to JobTracker:

  ```
  define command{
    command_name check_alive_nodes
    command_line $PATH$/check_hadoop_mapreduce_nodes.pl -H $HOSTADDRESS$ -P $PORT$ -n $ARG2$ -w $ARG3$ -c $ARG4$
  }

  define host {

    use hadoop-server
    host_name jt1
    alias Remote
    Host address 192.168.0.1
    contact_groups admins
  }
  Service definition:

  define service {

    use generic-service
    service_description mrnode_count
    contact_groups admins

    check_command check_alive_nodes
  }
  ```

- **Heap size of JobTracker**: Checks for the heap size used by JobTracker:

  ```
  define command{
    command_name check_jt_heap
    command_line $PATH$/check_hadoop_mapreduce_nodes.pl -H $HOSTADDRESS$ -P $PORT$ --heap-usage -w $ARG3$ -c $ARG4$
  }

  define host {

    use hadoop-server
    host_name jt1
    alias Remote
    Host address 192.168.0.1
    contact_groups admins
  }
  ```

Service definition:

```
define service {

  use generic-service
  service_description jt_heap
  contact_groups admins

  check_command check_jt_heap
}
```

- **TaskTracker check**: Checks the health of TaskTracker:

```
define command{
  command_name check_tasktracker
  command_line $PATH$/check_hadoop_tasktracker.pl $HOSTADDRESS$ $ARG1$ $ARG1$
}

define host {

  use hadoop-server
  host_name tt1
  alias Remote
  Host address 192.168.0.11
  contact_groups admins
}
Service definition:

define service {

  use generic-service
  service_description tasktracker
  contact_groups admins

  check_command check_tasktracker!100!90
}
```

> For further reference, refer to http://exchange.nagios.org/directory/Plugins/Others/check-Hadoop-tasktrackers/details.

Similarly, we can add checks for memory, CPU, and other components. You can refer to *Chapter 4*, *HDFS Checks*, for CPU and memory checks.

Nagios client configuration

Each node must have an NRPE plugin installed with the checks described earlier in `/usr/local/nagios/libexec` and the commands specified in `/usr/local/nagios/etc/nrpe.cfg`, shown as follows:

```
command[check_jt_heap]=/usr/local/nagios/libexec/check_hadoop_namenode.pl -H $HOSTADDRESS$ -u $USER8$ -P $PORT$ -b $ARG2$
```

```
command[check_tasktracker]=/usr/local/nagios/libexec/check_tasktracker
```

Similarly, entries need to be made for each of the checks to be executed on the nodes.

Summary

In this chapter, we looked at how to set up monitoring for MapReduce components like JobTracker, TaskTracker, number of active nodes for running jobs, and heap usage. In the next chapter, we will look at Hadoop metrics and visualizations with Ganglia.

6
Hadoop Metrics and Visualization Using Ganglia

In this chapter, we will look at the Hadoop metrics and visualization of various components like CPU, memory, and disk, by using Ganglia. This chapter is a build from the initial chapters on the monitoring and installation of Ganglia. Hadoop is a distributed platform with various services running across the cluster, which provides many metrics to tap into the Hadoop counters and other functional parameters.

In this chapter, we will look at the metrics for various Hadoop components.

The following topics will be covered in this chapter:

- Hadoop metrics contexts
- Metrics collection under DFS context
- Metrics collection under mapred context
- Metrics collection under RPC, JVM, and other contexts
- Visualizing the metrics with Ganglia

Hadoop metrics

In Hadoop, there are many daemons running, such as DataNode, NameNode, and JobTracker; each of these daemons captures a lot of information about the components they work on. Similarly, in the YARN framework, we have ResourceManager, NodeManager, and ApplicationManager, each of which exposes metrics, explained in the following sections under Metrics2. For example, DataNode collects metrics such as the number of blocks it has for advertising to the NameNode, the number of replicated blocks, and metrics about read/writes from clients. In addition to this, there could be metrics related to events, and so on. Hence, it is very important to gather them for the working of the Hadoop cluster and for debugging, if something goes wrong.

Therefore, Hadoop has a metrics system for collecting all this information. There are two versions of the metrics system, metrics and Metrics2 for Hadoop 1.x and Hadoop 2.x, respectively. The `hadoop-metrics.properties` and `hadoop-metrics2.properties` files for each Hadoop version can be configured.

Metrics contexts

Metrics are more relevant to the maintainers of the Hadoop clusters than its users. There might be many users who run MapReduce jobs on a cluster; they are concerned about MapReduce Counters and not the metrics, which are daemon specific. MapReduce counters talk about the number of mappers or reducers, number of bytes read or written to the HDFS and non-HDFS File System, how many spills happened, information about the shuffle phase, etc. However, for Hadoop administrators, metrics about the daemons are of more concern, in order to better understand the cluster.

Named contexts

Each of the daemons has a group of contexts for it. Some of the contexts, which are supported or rather available, are listed in the following table:

Hadoop 1.x	Hadoop 2.x
jvm: for Java Virtual Machine	**yarn**: for the YARN components
dfs: for Distributed File System	**jvm**: for Java Virtual Machine
mapred: for JobTracker and TaskTracker	**dfs**: for Distributed File System
rpc: for Remote Procedure Calls	**mapred**: for ResourceManager and NodeManager
	rpc: for Remote Procedure Calls

The metrics are collected by many Hadoop daemons in various metrics contexts. The daemons, which support metrics collection, are listed in the following table:

Hadoop 1.x daemons	Hadoop 2.x daemons
namenode	namenode
datanode	secondarynamenode
jobtracker	datanode
tasktracker	resourcemanager
maptask	nodemanager
reducetask	mrappmaster
	maptask
	reducetask

Metrics system design

Hadoop provides a framework to collect internal events and metrics and report them to the external system. The external system could be simply writing to a file or a tool like Ganglia. The new Hadoop Metrics2 framework has been revamped to integrate better with Ganglia.

The best things about the framework are the pluggable output plugins and the ability to reconfigure it without the need to restart the daemons.

The metrics have three main parts:

- **Producer**: The producer is the source of metrics generation and produces metrics for the upstream
- **Consumers**: They are basically the sinks of the framework, as they consume the metrics generated by the producers

- **Pollers**: They poll the sources and deliver data to the sink or consumers

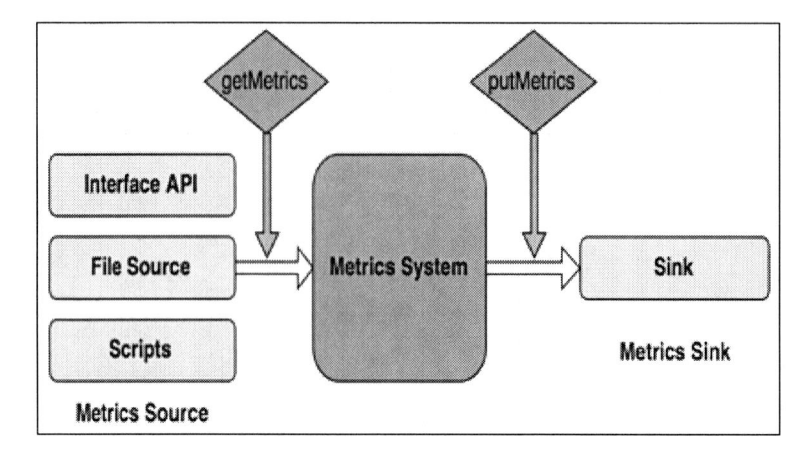

Metrics configuration

The Hadoop daemons expose runtime metrics, which can be collected using plugins. The old Metrics1 system has been replaced by the new Metrics2 system, which supports the following:

- Metrics collection using multiple plugins
- Better integration with JMX
- Better filters for cutting out noise

Before configuring metrics, it is important to understand which metrics and servlets are supported by each Hadoop version. For example, the servlet at **/metrics** works only with Metrics1 and the new servlet at **/jmx** works with both Metrics1 and Metrics2.

We need to configure a source, consumer, and poller for the framework:

- **Source or producer**: A metric source class must implement the following interface:

  `org.apache.hadoop.metrics2.MetricsSource`

- **Consumer or sink**: A consumer or sink must be implemented with the following line of code:

  `org.apache.hadoop.metrics2.MetricsSink`

For example, the configuration for JobTracker sink and filter is as follows:

```
jobtracker.sink.file.class=org.apache.hadoop.metrics2.sink.FileSink
jobtracker.sink.file.filename=jobtracker-metrics.out
```

We can filter based on source, context, and tags:

```
test.sink.file1.class=org.apache.hadoop.metrics2.sink.FileSink
test.sink.file0.context=foo:
```

Configuring Metrics2

For Hadoop version 2, which uses the YARN framework, the metrics can be configured using `hadoop-metrics2.properties`, in the $HADOOP_HOME folder:

```
*.sink.file.class=org.apache.hadoop.metrics2.sink.FileSink
*.period=10
namenode.sink.file.filename=namenode-metrics.out
datanode.sink.file.filename=datanode-metrics.out
jobtracker.sink.file.filename=jobtracker-metrics.out
tasktracker.sink.file.filename=tasktracker-metrics.out
maptask.sink.file.filename=maptask-metrics.out
reducetask.sink.file.filename=reducetask-metrics.out
```

We can also script it out and use it for metrics generation, shown as follows:

```
# namenode
[script://./bin/hadoop_metrics.sh http://192.168.1.70:50070/jmx]
disabled = 0
interval = 10
sourcetype = hadoop_metrics
index = hadoop_metrics

# datanode
[script://./bin/hadoop_metrics.sh http://192.168.1.70:50075/jmx]
disabled = 0
interval = 10
sourcetype = hadoop_metrics
index = hadoop_metrics

# jobtracker
[script://./bin/hadoop_metrics.sh http://192.168.1.70:50030/jmx]
```

```
disabled = 0
interval = 10
sourcetype = hadoop_metrics
index = hadoop_metrics
```

We can also use a file-based source input as follows:

```
[monitor://<absolute_path_to_namenode_metrics_output_file>]
disabled = 0
sourcetype=hadoop_metrics
index=hadoop_metrics

[monitor://<absolute_path_to_datanode_metrics_output_file>]
disabled = 0
sourcetype=hadoop_metrics
index=hadoop_metrics
```

Before using the file-based source, as mentioned previously, data must be dumped into a file so that it can be a consumer. We can do this by simply configuring `hadoop-metrics.properties` to use `FileContext`, as follows:

```
# Configuration of the "dfs" context for file
dfs.class=org.apache.hadoop.metrics.file.FileContext
dfs.period=10
# You'll want to change the path
dfs.fileName=/tmp/hdfsmetrics.log
# Configuration of the "mapred" context for file
mapred.class=org.apache.hadoop.metrics.file.FileContext
mapred.period=10
mapred.fileName=/tmp/map_reducemetrics.log
# Configuration of the "jvm" context for file
jvm.class=org.apache.hadoop.metrics.file.FileContext
jvm.period=10
jvm.fileName=/tmp/jvm_metrics.log
# Configuration of the "rpc" context for file
rpc.class=org.apache.hadoop.metrics.file.FileContext
rpc.period=10
rpc.fileName=/tmp/rpc_metrics.log
```

The files written previously, such as `rpc_metrics.log` and `mapreduce_metrics.log`, can act as the source for consumption by any system.

All the above discussed metrics can be a source for Ganglia or Splunk, which is another enterprise tool for collecting metrics and logs and scales very well for large datasets.

Exploring the metrics contexts

Till now, we have seen that there are various metrics contexts such as JVM, DFS, and RPC. Let's look at them and explore some of the examples, depicting what each context looks like and what it logs:

- **JVM context**: The JVM context contains stats about JVM memory, threads, heap memory, and so on:

    ```
    jvm.metrics: hostName=dn1.cluster1.com, processName=DataNode, sesionId=,logError=0,logFatal=0,logInfo=159,logWarn=0, memHeapCommittedM=9.4,memHeapUsedM=12.63,memNonHeapCommittedM=28.75,memNonHeapUsedM=19.7356,threadsBlocked=0, threadsNew=0, threadsRunnable=3, threadsTerminated=0, threadsTimedWaiting=2, threadsWaiting=1
    ```

- **DFS context**: The DFS context stats talk about the namenode files, capacity, blocks, and so on:

    ```
    dfs.FSNamesystem: hostName=nn1.cluster1.com, sessionId=, BlocksTotal=440, CapacityRemainingGB=100, CapacityTotalGB=254, CapacityUsedGB=0, FilesTotal=160, PendingReplicationBlocks=0, ScheduledReplicationBlocks=0, TotalLoad=1, UnderReplicatedBlocks=20
    ```

- **Mapred context**: This context talks about the stats for JobTracker and TaskTracker, such as the number of jobs submitted and the number of the tasks completed:

    ```
    mapred.jobtracker: hostName=jt.cluster1.com, sessionId=, jobs_completed=0, jobs_submitted=10, maps_completed=24, maps_launched=26, reduces_completed=4, reduces_launched=8
    mapred.tasktracker: hostName=dn1.cluster1.com, sessionId=, mapTaskSlots=6, maps_running=2, reduceTaskSlots=2, reduces_running=1, tasks_completed=24, tasks_failed_ping=0, tasks_failed_timeout=0
    ```

Hadoop Ganglia integration

Ganglia is a metrics collection and a visualization tool for the enterprise and works very well with Nagios and Hadoop. In addition to just collecting stats about CPU, memory, and disk, other finely tuned metrics are required, which can be provided by this framework.

Until now, we have seen that the metrics collection can be done to a file or to any other tool like Splunk, depending upon the class interface. We can configure which class handles the metrics update.

For Ganglia, we use `GangliaContext`, which is an implementation of `MetricsContext`. Ganglia versions higher than 3.0 provide this integration and work very well for collecting the Hadoop metrics.

In Ganglia, the metrics can be collected for NameNode, JobTracker, MapReduce tasks, JVM, RPC, DataNodes, and the new YARN framework.

Hadoop metrics configuration for Ganglia

Firstly, we need to define a sink class, as per Ganglia version 3.1:

```
*.sink.ganglia.class=org.apache.hadoop.metrics2.sink.ganglia.GangliaSink31
```

Secondly, we need to define the frequency of how often the source should be polled for data. We will poll every 30 seconds as follows:

```
*.sink.ganglia.period=30
```

Define retention for the metrics:

```
*.sink.ganglia.dmax=jvm.metrics.threadsBlocked=70,jvm.metrics.memHeapUsedM=40
```

Define the servers for various Hadoop daemons:

```
namenode.sink.ganglia.servers= gang.cluster1.com:8661
datanode.sink.ganglia.servers= gang.cluster1.com:8660
jobtracker.sink.ganglia.servers= gang.cluster1.com:8662
tasktracker.sink.ganglia.servers= gang.cluster1.com:8660
maptask.sink.ganglia.servers= gang.cluster1.com:8660
reducetask.sink.ganglia.servers= gang.cluster1.com:8660
```

Another important thing is to define the slope of Ganglia. It can take values such as zero, positive, negative, or both positive and negative.

```
*.sink.ganglia.slope=jvm.metrics.gcCount=zero,jvm.metrics.memHeapUsedM=both
```

The following table shows the values for the slope of the graphs:

Value	Description
Zero	The metrics value will always remain the same
Positive	The metrics value can only increase
Negative	The metrics value can only decrease
Both	The metrics value can both increase and decrease

Setting up Ganglia nodes

Now, let's configure Ganglia to talk to the Hadoop cluster, which spits out metrics, by using any of the methods mentioned previously.

We have already discussed the installation of Ganglia and its important components in *Chapter 1, Introduction to Monitoring*. Please refer to it if you need further details on configuration and architecture.

Ganglia mainly has `gmetad` as the main daemon and `gmond` runs on each node in the cluster and sends the stats to a collector as shown in the following diagram:

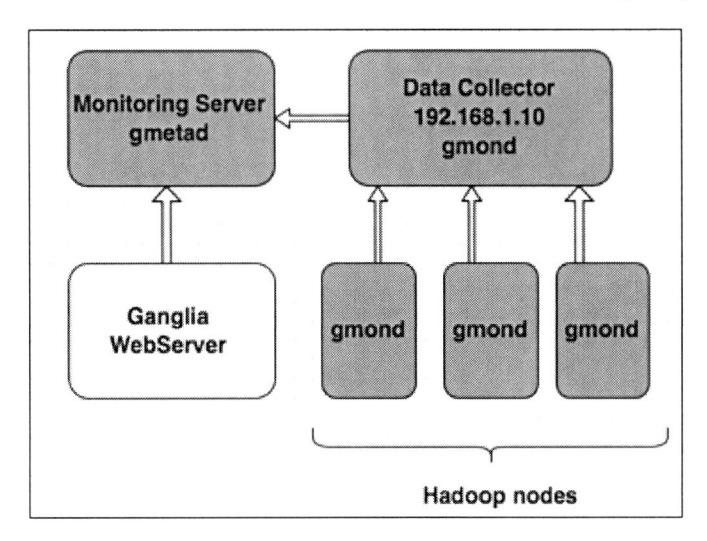

1. **On the monitoring server**: Configure the `/etc/ganglia/gmetad.conf` file to include the following line:

    `data_source "Hadoop" 192.168.1.10`

    where `192.168.1.10` is the IP address of **Data Collector**

2. **On the Data Collector node**: Configure the `/etc/ganglia/gmond.conf` file to include the following lines:

    ```
    cluster {
      name = "Hadoop"
      owner = "unspecified"
      latlong = "unspecified"
    ```

```
      url = "unspecified"
    }

    udp_recv_channel {
      port = 8649
      bind = 192.168.1.10
    }
```

3. **On all nodes in the Hadoop cluster**: Configure the `/etc/ganglia/gmond.conf` file to contain the following lines:

```
cluster {
  name = "Hadoop"
  owner = "unspecified"
  latlong = "unspecified"
  url = "unspecified"
}

udp_send_channel {
  host = 192.168.1.10
  port = 8649
}
```

Hadoop configuration

Now, we must set up the Hadoop Configuration file to point to the Ganglia servers.

Metrics1

Update the `hadoop-metrics.properties` file with the following lines:

```
dfs.class=org.apache.hadoop.metrics.ganglia.GangliaContext31
dfs.period=10
dfs.servers=192.168.1.10:8649

mapred.class=org.apache.hadoop.metrics.ganglia.GangliaContext31
mapred.period=10
mapred.servers=192.168.1.10:8649

jvm.class=org.apache.hadoop.metrics.ganglia.GangliaContext31
jvm.period=10
```

```
jvm.servers=192.168.1.10:8649

rpc.class=org.apache.hadoop.metrics.ganglia.GangliaContext31
rpc.period=10
rpc.servers=192.168.1.10:8649

ugi.class=org.apache.hadoop.metrics.ganglia.GangliaContext31
ugi.period=10
ugi.servers=192.168.1.10:8649
```

Metrics2

Update the `hadoop-metrics2.properties` file with the following lines:

```
namenode.sink.ganglia.class=org.apache.hadoop.metrics2.sink.ganglia.GangliaSink31
namenode.sink.ganglia.period=30
namenode.sink.ganglia.servers=192.168.1.10:8649

datanode.sink.ganglia.class=org.apache.hadoop.metrics2.sink.ganglia.GangliaSink31
datanode.sink.ganglia.period=30
datanode.sink.ganglia.servers=192.168.1.10:8649

jobtracker.sink.ganglia.class=org.apache.hadoop.metrics2.sink.ganglia.GangliaSink31
jobtracker.sink.ganglia.period=30
jobtracker.sink.ganglia.servers=192.168.1.10:8649

tasktracker.sink.ganglia.class=org.apache.hadoop.metrics2.sink.ganglia.GangliaSink31
tasktracker.sink.ganglia.period=30
tasktracker.sink.ganglia.servers=192.168.1.10:8649

maptask.sink.ganglia.class=org.apache.hadoop.metrics2.sink.ganglia.GangliaSink31
maptask.sink.ganglia.period=30
maptask.sink.ganglia.servers=192.168.1.10:8649

reducetask.sink.ganglia.class=org.apache.hadoop.metrics2.sink.ganglia.GangliaSink31
reducetask.sink.ganglia.period=30
reducetask.sink.ganglia.servers=192.168.1.10:8649
```

Ganglia graphs

Once the configuration is in place and the services have started, we can see the metrics being collected and plotted by using the Ganglia web interface, as shown in the following screenshot:

Let's have a look at the next screenshot:

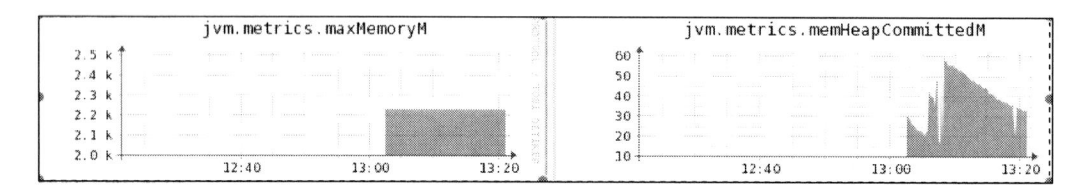

Metrics APIs

For reporting metrics, we have a package that provides APIs for both Metrics1 and Metrics2. It provides the flexibility to use client libraries and different modules from within an application.

The org.apache.hadoop.metrics package

This package provides sub-packages to do the specified task:

    org.apache.hadoop.metrics.spi

The abstract Server Provider Interface package. Those wishing to integrate the metrics API with a particular metrics client library should extend this package:

    org.apache.hadoop.metrics.file

An implementation package that writes the metric data to a file or sends it to the standard output stream:

`org.apache.hadoop.metrics.ganglia`

An implementation package that sends metrics data to Ganglia.

The new Metrics2 provides a lot more packages for the implementation.

The org.apache.hadoop.metrics2 package

- `org.apache.hadoop.metrics2.annotation`: This is the public annotation that interfaces for simpler metrics instrumentation.
- `org.apache.hadoop.metrics2.filter`: This is the built-in metrics filter that includes implementations such as GlobFilter and RegexFilter.
- `org.apache.hadoop.metrics2.source`: These are the built-in metrics that include source implementations such as JvmMetrics.
- `org.apache.hadoop.metrics2.sink`: These are the built-in metrics that include sink implementations such as FileSink.
- `org.apache.hadoop.metrics2.util`: These are the general utilities for implementing metrics sinks and so on, including the MetricsCache.

Summary

In this chapter, we looked at how to do metrics collections, the different metrics contexts and their groups, and the package APIs for integration with Ganglia for graphing the metrics. In the next chapter, we will look at the monitoring of some of the other components of Hadoop, such as Hive and HBase, and some performance improvement tips and tuning.

7
Hive, HBase, and Monitoring Best Practices

In this chapter, we will look at the monitoring and metrics collection for Hive, HBase, and many more. In addition to this, we will look at best practices for tuning Nagios and other improvements, which will be really helpful in large enterprise setups.

The chapter is a build from the previous chapter on metrics collection and monitoring covered in the initial chapters.

The following topics will be covered in this chapter:

- Hive monitoring
- HBase monitoring
- Metrics collections
- Tuning and improvements for large setups of clusters

Hive monitoring

In Hadoop, Apache Hive is a data warehousing tool, similar to SQL. It provides a query layer on top of Hadoop, thus easing out the learning curve between the traditional DBAs using SQL and the Hadoop framework.

In Apache Hive, the query language is referred to as HiveQL; it contains Metastore, which can be embedded, implying that it is internal and stored in the default database called `derby`, or stored externally in an RDMS such as MySQL. External storage is considered a best practice, as it lets multiple users connect to Hive. In the embedded mode, only one user can connect to the Hive prompt.

It is very important to make sure that Hive components such as Metastore or host health are constantly monitored. There are few important things that need to be kept track of in Hive such as the following:

- **Hive Metastore health checks**: Irrespective of whether Metastore is local or remote, it is important to monitor the health of Metastore. Important things to keep track of are as follows:
    - Number of open file descriptors
    - Basic checks such as client connectivity to Metastore; operations such as create database, create table, and create partitions; dropping tables and databases

- **Hive server health check**: The hosts hosting both the Hive clients and Metastores must have basic Nagios host checks in place as discussed in the earlier chapters. Metastore usually on MySQL must be monitored with MySQL Nagios checks. Also, make sure to check for the high availability of the Hive instances.

- **Hive log and scratch free space**: During the execution of Hive queries, a lot of logs are generated and a lot of temporary space is consumed for intermediate operations, which is usually referred to as temporary space; it must be monitored using the Nagios disk space check and cleaned regularly.

Hive metrics

Apache Hive provides very basic metrics for JVM profiling, which could be handy from the monitoring and performance aspects.

It makes sense to enable JMX when running the Hive thrift server by using the following code snippet:

```
JMX_OPTS="-Dcom.sun.management.jmxremote -Dcom.sun.management.jmxremote.authenticate=false -Dcom.sun.management.jmxremote.ssl=false -Dcom.sun.management.jmxremote.port=8008"
```

With the thrift server, it actually executes `hadoop jar` and passes the option to JVM; `$HIVE_OPTS` must be set in the `hive-env.sh` file.

The Java package called `org.apache.hadoop.hive.common.metrics` can be tapped for Hive metrics collection.

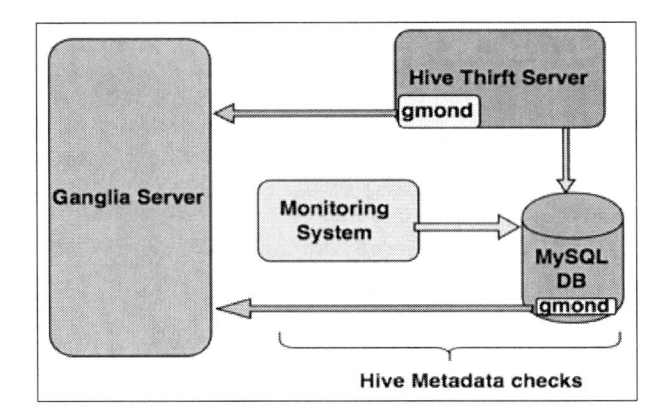

HBase monitoring

HBase is a NoSQL database designed to work very well on a distributed framework such as Hadoop. It has the concept of master and slave servers (region servers) much like the Hadoop architecture. Being a database and holding large amounts of data makes its state consistent and performance optimal.

Knowing what's happening at a given time can help spot problems, diagnose failures, and plan for expansion if needed. This can be achieved only if we have monitoring in place and are collecting metrics, which gives us an insight into what's going on with the system.

HBase Nagios monitoring

To monitor HBase master and region servers, there are Nagios plugins that can be downloaded from the `exchange.nagios.org` website and configured to monitor the HBase components. The plugins can be downloaded from https://github.com/harisekhon/nagios-plugins. As discussed in the earlier chapters, each check needs to be defined with a service on the Nagios master and a corresponding NRPE check must be configured on the client hosts. For example, the `check_hbase_tables_jsp.pl` check can be used to check for HBase connectivity and table states by using the JSP interface of the HBase server.

In addition to this, HBase comes with a tool called `hbase hbck`, which provides a lot of useful information about the state of the master and each region server. This command lists a lot of information about the tables; we can filter out the ROOT and META tables by using a custom plugin and use it to pull the status to Nagios.

As usual, first define a service for this in the Nagios server as follows and then configure an NRPE check on the client side:

```
define service {
  use                  generic-service
  host_name            HBase nodes
  service_description  Hbase check
  check_command        check_nrpe_1arg!check_hbase_state
}
```

On the HBase nodes, set up NRPE in the `/usr/local/nagios/etc/nrpe.conf` folder, and check as follows:

```
command[check_hbase_state]=/usr/lib/nagios/plugins/check_hbase_state
```

Copy the plugin from the `usr/local/nagios/libexec` folder on each of the HBase nodes.

The following screenshot shows the Nagios plugin output:

```
Current Status:        OK (for 2d 20h 6m 35s)
Status Information:    Ok. HBase is healthy.

                       Number of Tables: 6
                       Number of live region servers: 6
                       Number of dead region servers: 0
                       Number of empty REGIONINFO_QUALIFIER rows in .META.: 0
                       Summary:
                       Multiple table descriptors were found.
                       You can ignore it if your cluster is working fine.
                       To fix it, please re-run hbck with option -fixTableDesc

                       -ROOT- is okay.
                       Number of regions: 1
                       Deployed on: c1-s6.cluster:60020
                       .META. is okay.
                       Number of regions: 1
```

All other checks will be standard, such as checks for memory, CPU, disk, and system load. There is a tool called **Chukwa**, which is a data collection system for monitoring distributed systems. It is built on top of HDFS and MapReduce and scales very well. It falls under the Apache Software Foundation and can be used for analyzing and displaying data as shown in the next screenshot of load from a Chukwa graph. Chukwa is not in included in any distribution, but it can be downloaded and installed from `https://chukwa.apache.org/`.

CPU Utilization

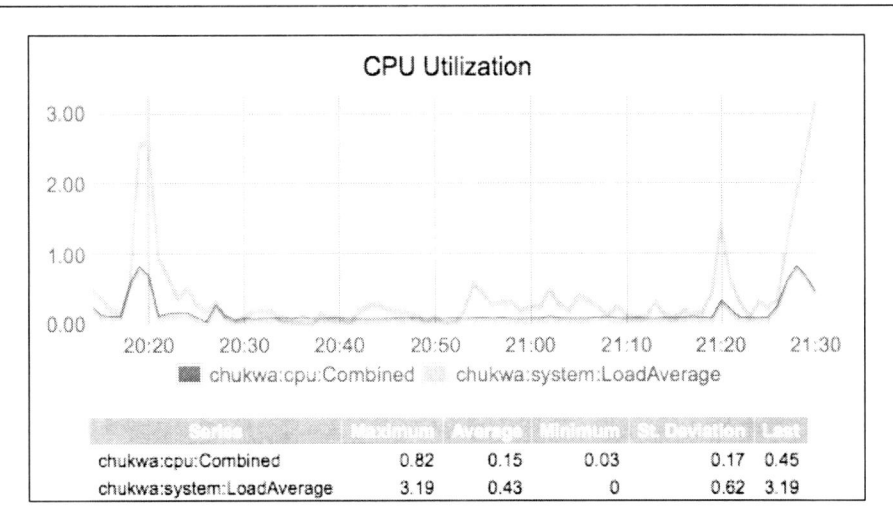

Series	Maximum	Average	Minimum	St. Deviation	Last
chukwa:cpu:Combined	0.82	0.15	0.03	0.17	0.45
chukwa:system:LoadAverage	3.19	0.43	0	0.62	3.19

HBase metrics

HBase provides an interface to tap into the various metrics that it provides. The new improved Metrics2 system has a lot of metrics for looking into how the HBase components perform. The main motivation behind any metrics collection is to understand the behavior of the system, debug any issues, or give us a forecast for our requirements.

The HBase master, region server has a Metrics2 system to tap into and look for minute details in terms of its memory, CPU, and I/O parameters.

We can get metrics from many components in the case of HBase, as shown in the following diagram:

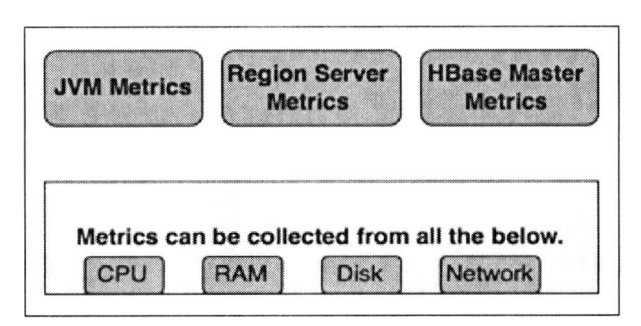

The collection method could be as simple as writing to a file or web UI or JMX or Ganglia. To collect metrics in any of the given forms, HBase must generate them first by using `hadoop-metrics.properties` by enabling the contexts per plugin.

These contexts could be RPC, region server-based, or JVM contexts; accordingly, the metrics will be generated either to a file or to the Ganglia `gmetd` daemon.

For region servers, it will show count on regions and store files and MemStore size. On Masters, it will show the cluster counts. The RPC and JVM contexts are useful for invocations, memory, number of threads, and so on.

The HBase stats can be collected by enabling JMX in the metrics properties file as discussed in the earlier chapters. For HBase, we can add the following lines to enable contexts:

```
hbase.class=org.apache.hadoop.metrics.spi.NullContextWithUpdateThread
hbase.period=60
hbase.class=org.apache.hadoop.metrics.ganglia.GangliaContext31
hbase.servers=hadoop-master.IP.address:8649
```

The IP address above will be of the `gmetad` server, which has been explained in the previous chapter. Secondly, we need to enable the JMX support in the `hbase-env.sh` file and restart HBase.

```
HBASE_JMX_OPTS="-Dcom.sun.management.jmxremote -Dcom.sun.management.jmxremote.ssl=false"
export HBASE_MASTER_OPTS="$HBASE_JMX_OPTS -Dcom.sun.management.jmxremote.port=10101"
export HBASE_REGIONSERVER_OPTS="$HBASE_JMX_OPTS -Dcom.sun.management.jmxremote.port=10102"
```

There are various metrics collection packages for each of the components. For example, the following table shows a few of the metrics available for a region server.

Region server metrics	Description
`hbase.regionserver.compactionQueueSize`	Size of the compaction queue
`hbase.regionserver.memstoreSizeMB`	Total memory storage size
`hbase.regionserver.regions`	Number of regions served by a region server
`hbase.regionserver.stores`	Number of stores on a region server
`hbase.regionserver.storeFiles`	Number of open HFile files per region server

Out of the many metrics available, the most important ones are requests and compaction queues for HBase; I/O wait and user CPU for OS; and **Garbage Collection** (GC) for Java. In addition to the slow query log, there are metrics for the slow query in the JMX context using `hadoop.regionserver_rpc_slowResponse` and `hadoop.regionserver_rpc_methodName.aboveOneSec`, which reflect the duration of responses that lasted for more than 1 second.

The following diagram shows the metrics collection system and the interface to the Java packages for it.

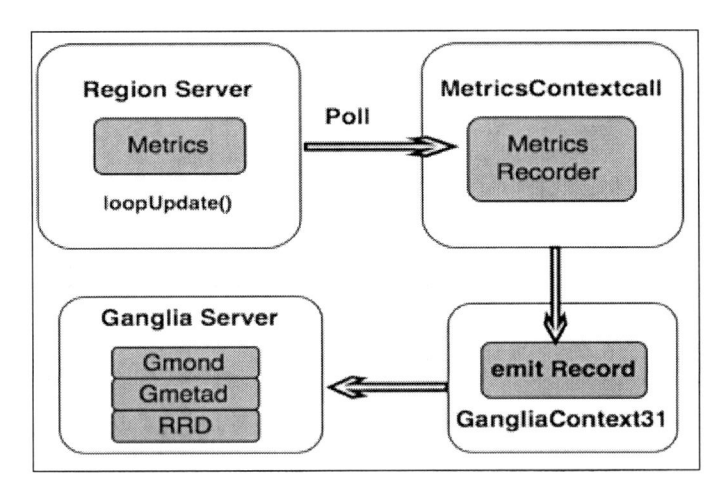

Monitoring best practices

Until now, we have talked about monitoring and metrics collection for Hadoop components, HBase, Hive, and many more. But, it is very important to understand what should be collected, else we might find it difficult to manage the data collected and extract any meaningful information from it.

It is good to enable logging, but at what level? Are we fine to log every event that is generated? Will that be helpful to us in any way? These are the questions we need to ask ourselves while designing a monitoring and logging system.

Some of the key points to keep in mind while designing a monitoring and metrics collection system are as follows:

- How easily it can be scaled
- How easily we can extract information from the system
- What we should log and collect
- How long should we keep the data

We cannot log or collect all the metrics; for example, let's say we have a 200-node cluster with HBase region servers. Let's say we collect 20 metrics per region, 500 regions live at a time, and we have around 2 million metrics emissions. If we are capturing them in Ganglia, many RRD files will be generated. This is a waste of resources, and until a feasible way of collecting data is developed, your Ganglia servers will have many files to plot.

The Filter class

To address the issue discussed above, Hadoop provides a `filter` class, which provides regular expressions to filter the metrics and make it more compact and meaningful as follows:

```
*.source.filter.class=org.apache.hadoop.metrics2.filter.GlobFilter
*.record.filter.class=${*.source.filter.class}
*.metric.filter.class=${*.source.filter.class}
```

The syntax of the `filter` class is explained as follows:

```
subsystem.[sink|source].sink_name.[sources|record|metric].filter.
[include|exclude]
subsystem - daemon: hbase, yarn, hdfs, etc
sink|source - sink or source for feed
sink_name - name of sink used
sources|record|metric - level of filter to operate
include|exclude - will filter exclude or include metrics.
```

The filters can be applied at the level of source, record, or metrics and constructed with regex for trimming the information generated by the metrics system.

Nagios and Ganglia best practices

To make sure that the monitoring and metrics collection system is working at the optimal performance, it must be designed and tuned for it.

- In the case of Nagios, make sure to have a right mix of active and passive checks for services.
- The performance of the total number of checks deployed as active checks and the number of nodes on which they will be executed, depends upon the resources that the Nagios server has in terms of memory and CPU cores.
- Also, the network plays an important role, as it important to understand how bandwidth monitoring will take place.

- Other best practice is to always have a hierarchy of the Nagios configuration layouts. Make use of host groups, service, and templates and having groups for everything makes adding nodes very easy.
- Define smart check rather than doing checks every minute. For example, doing a disk check every minute might not make sense, as it does not grow that often.
- Optimize plugins so as to reduce the load on the system. Use binary plugins wherever possible or use an embedded Perl interpreter. For customer plugins, try to provide command line arguments rather than having the plugin fetch it during runtime.
- Use RAM disks for maintaining the state of active checks and other temporary data, rather than writing to disk.
- Similarly for Ganglia, make sure what metrics are collected. Ganglia will capture all the metrics thrown at it, but this does not mean that we need all the metrics.
- The gmond daemons on each node can consume a lot of memory, so it is important to tune all our checks and data collections.
- For Ganglia, every hostname is a new machine, therefore make sure that the DNS resolution is fine and IP addresses do not change for machines.

Summary

In this chapter, we looked at how to monitor Hive, HBase, and their metrics collection. We also looked at the best monitoring practices for the enterprise, in addition to the filtering of alerts.

Index

A

Apache Hive. *See* Hive
Apache HTTP Server version 2.0 4

C

Chukwa
 about 70
 URL 70
configuration files, Nagios
 cgi.cfg 7
 commands.cfg 8
 contacts.cfg 8
 localhost.cfg 8
 resource.cfg 7
 nagios.cfg 7
control commands, MapReduce
 about 46, 47
 hadoop jobtracker -dumpConfiguration 47
 hadoop queue <options> 47
 yarn daemonlog -setlevel <host:port>
   <name> <level> 48
 yarn logs -applicationId <app Id>
   <options> 47
 yarn node <options> 47
 yarn rmadmin -checkHealth <serviceId> 48

D

DataNode
 about 19
 parameters 19
derby 67
DFS context 59
DRFA (Daily Rolling File Appender) 35

F

filter class 74

G

Ganglia
 about 11, 59
 best practices 74, 75
 components 11
 download link 12
 features 11
 graphs 64
 installing 12, 13
Ganglia Meta Daemon (gmetad) 12
Ganglia Monitoring Daemon (gmond) 11
Ganglia nodes
 configuring 61
 configuring, on Hadoop cluster
   nodes 62
 configuring, on Data Collector node 61
 configuring, on monitoring server 61
Garbage Collection (GC) 73

H

Hadoop 1.0 18
Hadoop 2.0 18
Hadoop configuration
 Metrics1 62
 Metrics2 63
 performing 62
Hadoop daemons
 about 18
 communication, between daemons 21, 22
 DataNode 19

JobTracker 20
NameNode 18
secondary NameNode 20
TaskTracker 19
YARN daemons 20
hadoop dfsadmin -report command 38
hadoop fsck / command 38
hadoop fs -count -q / command 38
hadoop fs -dus command 38
Hadoop Ganglia integration
about 59
Ganglia nodes, setting up 61
Hadoop metrics configuration 60
Hadoop logs
about 33
error logs 33
Hadoop daemon logs 33
job logs 33
Log4j 33
logging format 33
parameters 34
Hadoop metrics 54
Hadoop metrics configuration, for Ganglia
performing 60
retention for metrics, defining 60
servers for Hadoop daemons, defining 60
HBase metrics
about 71, 72
region server metrics 72
HBase Nagios monitoring 69, 70
HDFS 38
HDFS checks
about 37, 38
Nagios client configuration 43
Nagios master configuration 39
HDFS space check 39
high availability (HA) 48
Hive
about 67
HBase monitoring 69
metrics 68
monitoring 67
Hive log and scratch free space 68
Hive Metastore health checks 68
Hive server health check 68

J

JobTracker
about 20
parameters 20
jps command 38
JVM context 59

L

logging. *See* **system logging**
logging events
accountability 30
intrusion detection 30
need for 30
problem detection 30
logging, Hadoop
about 32
audit 35
Log4j.properties 35
log level 34, 35
logging levels
about 31, 32
facilities 31
priorities 31
log management challenges, Hadoop
analysis 33
excessive logging 32
retention 33
truncation 32

M

Mapred context 59
MapReduce
control commands 46, 47
health checks 48
overview 46
MapReduce checks
about 45
Nagios client configuration 52
Nagios master configuration 48
metrics
configuring 56
consumer, configuring 56
producer, configuring 56

sink, configuring 56
source, configuring 56
Metrics2
  configuring 57, 58
Metrics APIs
  about 64
  org.apache.hadoop.metrics2 package 65
  org.apache.hadoop.metrics package 64
metrics contexts
  about 54
  DFS context 59
  exploring 59
  JVM context 59
  Mapred context 59
  named contexts 54
metrics system design
  about 55
  consumers 55
  pollers 56
  producer 55
mnode 39
monitoring
  about 1
  best practices 73, 74
  need for 2
monitoring tools
  BandwidthD 2
  EasyNetMonitor 2
  Ganglia 11
  Nagios 3
  NetXMS 2
  Splunk 2
  Zenoss 2
MRv2 47

N

Nagios
  about 3
  architecture 3
  best practices 74, 75
  configuration files 7, 8
  configuring 3
  download link, for plugin 39
  features 3
  installing 3, 4
  monitoring, setting up for clients 8-11
  plugins 7
  URL 4
  verification 7
  web interface configuration 5, 6
Nagios client configuration, HDFS checks 43
Nagios client configuration, MapReduce checks 52
Nagios master configuration, HDFS checks
  HDFS balancer, checking 40
  HDFS DataNode, counting 41
  HDFS replication, checking 40
  HDFS space check 39
  NameNode heap usage, checking 42
  Zookeeper, checking 42
Nagios master configuration, MapReduce checks
  about 48, 49
  heap size of JobTracker 50
  JobTracker health check 49
  number of alive nodes 50
  TaskTracker check 51
NameNode
  about 18
  parameters 18
NRPE addon
  URL 8

O

org.apache.hadoop.metrics2 package
  about 65
  org.apache.hadoop.metrics2.annotation 65
  org.apache.hadoop.metrics2.filter 65
  org.apache.hadoop.metrics2.sink 65
  org.apache.hadoop.metrics2.source 65
  org.apache.hadoop.metrics2.util 65
org.apache.hadoop.metrics package 64

S

secondary NameNode
  about 20
  parameters 20

system logging
  about 14, 30
  alerting 14
  analysis 14
  collection 14
  facility 15
  priority 15
  rsyslogd daemons 15
  storage 14
  syslogd daemons 15
  transportation 14

T

TaskTracker 19
TCO (Total Cost of Ownership) 2

Y

YARN (Yet Another Resource Negotiator)
  about 23
  common issues, on Hadoop cluster 24, 25
  Hadoop nodes, configuring for
      monitoring 27, 28
  host level checks 25
  Nagios server 26, 27

Thank you for buying
Monitoring Hadoop

About Packt Publishing

Packt, pronounced 'packed', published its first book, *Mastering phpMyAdmin for Effective MySQL Management*, in April 2004, and subsequently continued to specialize in publishing highly focused books on specific technologies and solutions.

Our books and publications share the experiences of your fellow IT professionals in adapting and customizing today's systems, applications, and frameworks. Our solution-based books give you the knowledge and power to customize the software and technologies you're using to get the job done. Packt books are more specific and less general than the IT books you have seen in the past. Our unique business model allows us to bring you more focused information, giving you more of what you need to know, and less of what you don't.

Packt is a modern yet unique publishing company that focuses on producing quality, cutting-edge books for communities of developers, administrators, and newbies alike. For more information, please visit our website at www.packtpub.com.

About Packt Open Source

In 2010, Packt launched two new brands, Packt Open Source and Packt Enterprise, in order to continue its focus on specialization. This book is part of the Packt Open Source brand, home to books published on software built around open source licenses, and offering information to anybody from advanced developers to budding web designers. The Open Source brand also runs Packt's Open Source Royalty Scheme, by which Packt gives a royalty to each open source project about whose software a book is sold.

Writing for Packt

We welcome all inquiries from people who are interested in authoring. Book proposals should be sent to author@packtpub.com. If your book idea is still at an early stage and you would like to discuss it first before writing a formal book proposal, then please contact us; one of our commissioning editors will get in touch with you.

We're not just looking for published authors; if you have strong technical skills but no writing experience, our experienced editors can help you develop a writing career, or simply get some additional reward for your expertise.

Mastering Hadoop

ISBN: 978-1-78398-364-3   Paperback: 374 pages

Go beyond the basics and master the next generation of Hadoop data processing platforms

1. Learn how to optimize Hadoop MapReduce, Pig and Hive.
2. Dive into YARN and learn how it can integrate Storm with Hadoop.
3. Understand how Hadoop can be deployed on the cloud and gain insights into analytics with Hadoop.

Hadoop MapReduce Cookbook

ISBN: 978-1-84951-728-7   Paperback: 300 pages

Recipes for analyzing large and complex datasets with Hadoop MapReduce

1. Learn to process large and complex data sets, starting simply, then diving in deep.
2. Solve complex big data problems such as classifications, finding relationships, online marketing and recommendations.
3. More than 50 Hadoop MapReduce recipes, presented in a simple and straightforward manner, with step-by-step instructions and real world examples.

Please check www.PacktPub.com for information on our titles

Learning Hadoop 2

ISBN: 978-1-78328-551-8　　　　Paperback: 382 pages

Design and implement data processing, lifecycle management, and analytic workflows with the cutting-edge toolbox of Hadoop 2

1. Construct state-of-the-art applications using higher-level interfaces and tools beyond the traditional MapReduce approach.
2. Use the unique features of Hadoop 2 to model and analyze Twitter's global stream of user generated data.
3. Develop a prototype on a local cluster and deploy to the cloud (Amazon Web Services).

Hadoop Beginner's Guide

ISBN: 978-1-84951-730-0　　　　Paperback: 398 pages

Learn how to crunch big data to extract meaning from the data avalanche

1. Learn tools and techniques that let you approach big data with relish and not fear.
2. Shows how to build a complete infrastructure to handle your needs as your data grows.
3. Hands-on examples in each chapter give the big picture while also giving direct experience.

Please check www.PacktPub.com for information on our titles

CPSIA information can be obtained
at www.ICGtesting.com
Printed in the USA
FFOW02n1831060715
14868FF